C000071643

TRAVEL I

CROATIA

By
LINDSAY BENNETT

Written by Lindsay Bennett
Updated by Robin Gauldie
Original photography by Pete Bennett

Editing and page layout by Cambridge Publishing Management Ltd,
Unit 2, Burr Elm Court, Caldecote CB23 7NU
Series Editor: Karen Beaulah

Published by Thomas Cook Publishing
A division of Thomas Cook Tour Operations Ltd
Company Registration No. 1450464 England

PO Box 227, The Thomas Cook Business Park,
Coningsby Road, Peterborough
PE3 8SB, United Kingdom
E-mail: books@thomascook.com
www.thomascookpublishing.com
Tel: +44 (0)1733 416477

ISBN: 978-1-84157-690-9

Text © 2007 Thomas Cook Publishing
Maps © 2007 Thomas Cook Publishing

First edition © 2002 Thomas Cook Publishing
Second edition © 2005 Thomas Cook Publishing
Third edition © 2007 Thomas Cook Publishing

Project Editor: Sasha Heseltine
Production/DTP Editor: Steven Collins

Printed and bound in Italy by: Printer Trento.

Front cover credits: © Johanna Huber/4 Corners Images, © Thomas Cook,
© Giuseppe Dall'Arche/4 Corners Images
Back cover credits: © Thomas Cook, © Thomas Cook

Contents

KEY TO MAPS

◎ Amphitheatre   🏛 Museum

𝕊 Ancient walls   ♣ Park

🛉 Church   ★ Start of walk

Introduction

If there were ingredients to create the perfect holiday destination, they might well include hours of sunshine, a tapestry of landscapes, carefree relaxation, epochs of history, an accumulation of culture, plenty of activities, a warm welcome – and a touch of spice! Of course, the ideal holiday is a matter of taste – a little extra relaxation for some, more sightseeing for others – but it is fair to say that the recipes for most locations are weighted: a city towards museums and a Caribbean island towards beaches, for example. However, Croatia has each of the ingredients for that perfect break in abundance. It is one of the most versatile destinations around, and long hot summer days provide the ideal backdrop to whatever you plan to do – whether nothing at all or lots.

The main draw is the sublime Adriatic coastline – the turquoise waters and golden shores – but here is where the country keeps its best secret. Croatia has no less than 1,777km (1,110 miles) of Adriatic mainland coastline, and a

Harbourside cafés are a favourite haunt

total of 4,058km (2,536 miles) when you count all the islands lying just offshore! Not just a beach for every day of the year, but a beach for each summer visitor. There's also a choice of intimate rocky coves or lively strands, swimsuit or birthday suit.

There is plenty of history for those with a thirst for culture. Croatia sat at the crossroads between western and eastern Rome (later the boundary between Catholic and Orthodox Christianity), and between Christianity and Islam. Politically it saw rule by generations of feudal duchies, medieval republics and empires from the north and the east. Each wanted to leave their mark – and many did, most tantalisingly in the august medieval and Renaissance enclaves that line the coast.

There is no prescribed tourist trail here, however. You don't have to squeeze yourself into the cramped itinerary of a pre-set tour. Simply hop on one of the vast fleet of ferries to the nearest offshore island, and *voilà* – you've created your own bespoke excursion. Or better still, let the sea breezes fill the

sails of your yacht so you can set course for your own secret anchorage.

Want to get active? Croatia is one of the best places in Europe for snorkelling, hiking, cycling or free climbing, and you can enjoy stupendous unspoilt landscapes while you're out and about. The country prides itself on its amazing range of national parks, which protect a range of environments from the dramatic limestone caverns to languid river deltas. And if complete relaxation is top of your agenda, put yourself in the hands of Croatia's 'wellness' specialists – they've been in business since the Roman era.

Whatever your pleasure, nothing is too much trouble for your hosts, who seem to go out of their way to welcome visitors. Despite their close historical contacts with the Italian peninsula, they don't display the fiery Latin temperament of their neighbours, though they love the café lifestyle of the *piazza*. Approachable, calm and unruffled, they have a natural *joie de vivre* typified by the vibrant traditional folk dances featured at summer festivals across the country.

And the spice? Well, the language is a challenge for all but the most adept polyglot. With three distinct dialects it can also be a bit of a test for the locals, but even here the amenable Croatians meet you halfway. English is widely spoken, so you don't have to carry a briefcase-sized phrase book to make yourself understood!

There are miles of unspoilt coastline to enjoy

Land and people

Our beautiful homeland
O so fearless and gracious
Our fathers' ancient glory
May you be blessed forever

Dear, you are our only glory
Dear, you are our only one
Dear, we love your plains
Dear, we love your mountains

Sava, Drava, keep on flowing
Danube do not lose your vigour
Deep blue sea, tell the world
That a Croat loves his homeland

While not the most-played anthem at events such as the Olympics, these first stanzas of the national anthem say so much about the highlights of Croatia or – to call it by its official name – the Republika Hrvatska. It praises the elemental natural phenomena that have fashioned the landscape and continue to influence the contemporary lifestyle.

Croatia is a country with an unusual shape. In the south, Dalmatia cuts a long, rapier-like thrust down the western Balkan Peninsula. At the top of this 'mast', like a flag flying eastwards from a pole, lies the landlocked parts of Croatia, including regions such as Slavonia and Baranja. In the northwest, Istria hangs like a pennant down into the Adriatic.

The country's relationship with the sea has been its most enduring and its most profitable. Where its land boundaries have been malleable, altered by the ebb and flow of various political powers through the centuries, the Adriatic has remained an indomitable ally; its safest transport system and its surest source of food. The Adriatic seaboard is Croatia's most public face. Hundreds of offshore islands, tiny fishing villages, sublime Renaissance palaces and fortified citadels draw the crowds.

But it's the limestone substrate and lack of surface water (no rivers or streams) that create the conditions for the traditional lifestyles that make Dalmatia unique: low-growing vegetation; a patchwork of limestone walls behind which sheep or vines are raised, safe from the worst effects of the *bora* wind; white rocks in the coastal shallows that reflect sunlight back through the water, giving us the azure

many of the islands, while a mixture of scrub and aromatic wild herbs conquer windblown crests and gullies. The Adriatic is the natural environment of the seabird – gulls of all sizes, shearwaters – as well as griffon vultures and other creatures: playful dolphins, octopus and an array of fish.

A ridge of dramatic jagged peaks, the Paklenica and Risnjak ranges, forms the watershed between coastal and continental Croatia. Not very high by international standards – the highest is Mt Dinara at 1,830m (6,007ft); nevertheless their stark limestone ridges, rising almost directly from the sea, make for dramatic scenery, as well as offering a haven for a number of rare species, from birds of prey to bears.

Once over the 'great divide', Croatia presents a second, totally contrasting face. The Pannonian Plain is a vast steppe, stretching on

hues that are so beloved of travel photographers. Soft fruits and fragrant flowers thrive here, though the olive is king. The heady scent of pine emanates from the dense forest that blankets

Croatia's azure sea

through the country's border and into the central Balkans. This is the agricultural heartland of the country. Maize, wheat and beet, cabbages, potatoes and apples grow in carefully tended plots – this is not yet the domain of the large, mechanised farm. The vast oak forests that once blanketed the plain are now being pushed to the uncultivated margins, though swathes now lie protected in national parks.

Water plays an important role in the ecosystem here also, but this time it's fresh water. Croatia's mighty rivers, the Drava and the Sava, mark her northern and southern borders, rolling inexorably on to their appointment with the Danube,

where Croatia gives way to Serbia. These rivers are some of the last untamed watercourses in Europe, rising and falling with the seasonal rainfall, flooding when nature dictates; acting as safety valves for the vast Danube basin and offering a habitat to myriad species of plants, fish, birds, insects and larger animals such as deer and wild boar.

NOBODY'S FAULT

Croatia sits on the edge of a continental fault line that makes it prone to earthquakes. Serious ones such as the 1667 Dubrovnik quake are thankfully rare. However, smaller quakes happen quite regularly, the last in 1996, while minor tremors are an accepted fact of everyday life.

Dramatic limestone peaks characterise the northern Dalmatian coast

People

Almost 4.5 million people live in Croatia, but the population balance has changed quite dramatically since before the conflict of the 1990s. Many of the Serbs born here have not returned since the cessation of hostilities (many of the empty houses you will see as you travel around the country belong to Serbs either killed in the fighting or displaced by it), leaving the ethnic mix at 89 per cent Croat, 4.5 per cent Serb, with others – mostly of Balkan descent – making up the balance.

The religious balance has changed somewhat too, as the mainly Christian Orthodox Serbs have dropped in number. Today 88 per cent of the population is Roman Catholic, while 4.5 per cent is Orthodox Christian. Even now, three quite separate dialects are spoken around the country, reflecting the differing backgrounds and histories of the peoples. The people speak Štokavski, Čakavski or Kajkavski depending on where they were born, but Štokavski has had most influence on modern spoken Croatian. In Istria, which was under Italian rule until the 20th century, a strong Italian accent is still audible in the speech.

Thomas Cook Travellers Croatia

This book is divided into a number of 'What to See' chapters. The capital Zagreb and the region of Istria each have a section devoted to them; a shorter chapter looks at Kvarner, an administrative region that covers the land and islands at the head of the Rijeki zaljev, east of Istria. Two chapters look at the abundant treasures of Dalmatia: one covers the north with its leading city of Split; the other the south, anchored by Dubrovnik. Finally, continental Croatia is divided into two sections: the north, easily visited from Zagreb, and the central and eastern plains, where the borders follow every curve of the sinuous courses of the Drava, Sava and Danube.

THE CROATIAN NATIONAL FLAG

The flag is three bands (red, white and blue), symbolising the national revival spirit – the three colours formed the uniform of the Viceroy of Croatia on his inauguration in 1848. The Croatian coat of arms is in the middle of the flag, a chequered red and white shield topped by five small shields. These small shields show the oldest Croatian coat of arms, the coat of arms of Ragusa, the Dalmatian coat of arms, the Istrian coat of arms and the Slavonian coat of arms, first displayed in the 15th century and marking a continuity through the ages.

Croatia's national flag flies proudly from public buildings

History

At a crossroads between peoples, ideas and religions since the dawn of human history, the influence of occupying empires on this part of the world is still evident. The twists and turns in Croatia's history are many; the list that follows highlights just some of the major events in the nation's lifespan.

c1300 BC–
750 BC
Illyric peoples from the east settle in Croatia.

229 BC
Croatian lands are annexed by the Romans.

AD 284
Illyric descendant Diocletian becomes Emperor of Rome. He builds a spectacular palace in Split.

400–600
The Byzantines and Slavs come into conflict over lands in the Balkans. Boundaries are in a constant state of flux.

7th
century
Croatian tribes from the east – probably Persia – arrive on the Dalmatian plain. They found the first organised, though small, state. Meanwhile, Byzantium rules the coast.

852
Prince Trpimir issues a document naming 'the Croats' as a 'people' for the first time. He invites the Roman Christian Church into his lands rather than the Eastern Byzantine Church.

879
Pope John VIII blesses the ruler of the Croats, officially recognising the Croat kingdom.

887
Croat naval victory over the Venetians in the Adriatic.

926
Bishop Grgur Ninski defies the Pope and preaches in Croatian rather than Latin.

1102–
1526
Croatia and Hungary come together in a common kingdom with a Sabor (parliament) and counties overseen by the nobility. Free cities are founded, forming a backbone of trade and defence. Along the coast, many ports have trading agreements with Venice.

13th
century
Venice begins a concerted effort to take the remaining areas of the

Magnificent Venetian façade

Croatian coast by force.
Zadar is plundered in
1202. Dubrovnik falls
to Venice in 1205.

1308 The Counts of Anjou
come to the Croat-
Hungarian throne.

1358 King Louis defeats the
Venetians, bringing the
coast within the larger
Croat/Hungarian kingdom.

1382 Dubrovnik gains
independence from the
kingdom and forms the
Republic of Ragusa.

1409 The Count of Anjou sells
Dalmatia (excluding
Ragusa) to the Venetians.

1526 The King of Hungary
and Croatia, Louis II,
is killed in battle.
The Ottoman Sultan
Suleyman the Magnificent
takes a large part of
southern Croatia.

1527 The Counts of Anjou cede
their remaining territory
to Archduke Ferdinand
of Habsburg.

1640– The Turks are pushed
1700 south out of the territory
during several campaigns.
In 1671, a Croat push for
self-determination is
brutally put down by
the Habsburgs.

1808 Napoleon's forces capture
the coastal towns.
They are renamed
the Illyrian Provinces.

1815 After Napoleon's demise,
the Illyrian Provinces and
Dubrovnik come under
Habsburg control.

1848 Hungary rises up against
Vienna, and the Austro-
Hungarian empire – in
which Hungary has more
autonomy – is forged.
There are more calls
for Croatian self-
determination.

1862 Serbia frees itself from Ottoman rule, becoming an independent country. It hopes to create a pan-Slav state in the Balkans.

1868 Croatia achieves more autonomy within the Austro-Hungarian empire with an administrative, political and cultural centre at Zagreb.

1914 The Austro-Hungarian empire enters World War I on the German side.

1918 After the war, the Austro-Hungarian empire is broken up. The kingdom of Serbs, Croats and Slovenes is created, though much of the coast is ceded to Italy.

1929 In Belgrade, King Alexander abolishes the 1918 constitution and creates the kingdom of Yugoslavia.

1934 King Alexander is assassinated in Marseille by Croat Fascists.

1939–45 As World War II rages, Yugoslavia allies itself with the Axis powers (Germany, Italy and Japan), but a military coup removes Prince Paul and the country is invaded by German forces. A short-lived Croat state is declared. Two bands of freedom fighters – communists under Josip Broz Tito and the mainly Serbian Chetniks – set up resistance. Tito's partisans are recognised by the Allies as the official opposition during the Tehran Conference.

1945 Tito consolidates his power base as the Axis collapses. Yugoslavia (complete with territory ceded to Italy after World War I) becomes a communist state.

1945–53 Tito takes an independent role in relations with Moscow; he pursues a non-aligned path, attached neither to the Soviet bloc nor to the West. Croatia becomes one of six republics in Tito's Yugoslavia, the others being Serbia, Slovenia, Bosnia-Herzegovina, Macedonia and Montenegro.

1974 Tito is elected president for life. He relaxes centralised control on industry and agriculture,

The scars of conflict are evident in east Croatia

but this creates rivalry between the republics, sowing the seeds for later problems. Nationalist and separatist movements grow in popularity within Yugoslavia.

1980s After the death of Tito in May 1980, the republics begin to divide along age-old nationalist, religious and ethnic lines.

1990 Free elections in Croatia see Tuđman's conservative nationalist party (HDZ) take the most seats.

1991 Civil war breaks out between the Serb and Croat populations, made worse by the intervention of Serbia itself. Dubrovnik is subjected to an eight-month siege by the Serbian army, suffering serious damage. Serbs 'ethnically cleanse' eastern Croatia of Croats. The EU recognises Croat independence.

1992 Fighting spreads to other republics, notably Bosnia. Slobodan Milošević's Serbians make great gains in power and territory but the UN intervenes.

1995 Peace is declared in the northern Yugoslavia region (including Croatia) after NATO air strikes against the Serbs.

1998 The last Serb army units leave Croat land under a UN supervised action.

1999 Death of Tuđman.

2000 Stjepan Mesić is elected president of Croatia. In November 2003 Dr Ivo Sanader is appointed prime minister.

2004 Croatia receives positive feedback on meeting EU concordance criteria.

2006 Croatian Prime Minister Ivo Sanader states that Croatia will be the 28th country to join the EU, probably during 2009.

The Habsburgs

One of the principal ruling dynasties in Europe, the Habsburgs survived from the early 14th to the 20th century, and have had a major influence in the shaping of our modern world.

The antecedents of the family are shrouded in mystery, but some claim they were descended from the Carolingians, a noble family of central France. Werner became the first Count of Habsburg in the 11th century (the family name is taken from their home castle, the Habichtsburg, or Hawks Castle, on the Aare River in what is now Switzerland). However, it was when – in 1273, on the orders of Pope Gregory X – Count Rudolph of Habsburg was crowned Rudolph I, German and Holy Roman Emperor, that the family really rose to prominence. The Pope needed Rudolph's money and support for a new Crusade; other European nobles had not greeted the idea with enthusiasm.

Rudolph I was a sharp operator. He consolidated his wealth and influence, acquiring duchies – an important unit of feudal power at a time when national governments

Habsburg majesty is depicted in stone on this building

had yet to evolve – in central Europe, particularly in Austria. These he made into hereditary fiefdoms, an unusual move at the time. Austria was to become the central core of the Habsburg empire.

Maximilian I (1459–1519) began the successful policy of using dynastic marriages to increase the Habsburg sphere of influence. He married into the Burgundian line in France, and his son, Philip (1478–1506), married the Infanta Joanna to bring Aragon and Castile (now Spain) on board. The zenith of the dynasty was the reign of Charles V (1500–58): it was said that the sun never set on his lands. During his rule, powerful duchies such as Sicily and Milan fell under the Habsburg sphere of influence, followed by whole countries including the Netherlands and Spain (along with all their attendant New World colonies).

Charles abdicated in 1556 and split the empire, leaving his westerly domains to his son, Philip II (1527–98). The easterly lands (Austria, Hungary and Bohemia) were passed to his brother Ferdinand (1503–64). However, from this point, with a few exceptions, the empire began to decline. The male Habsburg line in the west died out in 1700, which led to the Spanish War of Succession (1701–14). The male line of Austrian Habsburgs died out with Charles VI in 1740, but his daughter, the Habsburg Princess Maria Theresa (1717–80), married Francis of Lorraine, passing the title of Holy Roman Emperor to him.

Maria Theresa's grandson, Francis II (1768–1835), played a key role in opposing Napoleon (who was in essence trying to take Habsburg lands), but could not re-establish the monarchy. As the ramifications of the French Revolution played out during the 1800s, the family was forced from Italy and Germany. An uprising in Hungary led to the establishment of the Austro-Hungarian 'dual monarchy', further dividing and diluting the power of the Habsburgs.

In World War I, the Habsburgs were key allies of Germany's Kaiser Wilhelm; Germany's defeat brought their influence to an ignominious end. The victorious powers wanted to break up the empire, and a whole plethora of nationalist and ethnic groups pushed for self-determination. Charles I (1887–1922), Emperor of Austria and King of Hungary (1916–18), refused to recognise the new republic at home and went into exile, though he made two attempts to regain his throne. In 1961 Charles's son Otto was granted leave to apply to become an ordinary citizen of Austria. He later went on to settle in West Germany and was elected to the European parliament.

Politics

'In ancient times, the walls of Dubrovnik were inscribed with the Latin inscription Non bene pro toto libertas venditur auro *(freedom should not be sold for all the gold in the world). I think that you will agree that there is no more fitting location in Europe than this city to consider the democratic revolution that continues to advance freedom in southeast Europe and to transform our societies.'*

Ivo Sanadar, Croatian Prime Minister, 11 July 2006.

Croatia was the most proactive of Yugoslavia's regions and the first to declare itself independent from the communist state in 1991, triggering a rapid descent into bloody civil war. To briefly summarise a very complex situation, Croat boundaries contained a minority Serb population who had lived amongst the Croats for centuries. It was allegations of mistreatment of these Serbs (both physically and constitutionally) that brought Serbian and Yugoslav forces into conflict with the Croats and resulted in the invasion of Croatia. The conflict finally ended in 1995.

Today Croatia is a country still being forged from the crucible of that conflict. In this very new country with a long history, the government faces many challenges over the coming decade, both economic and social. Peace has been restored and violence denounced on all sides, but many strands still need to be put in place to draw together minority communities and restore their confidence. On a more mundane level, the country's infrastructure needs major investment, especially in the areas hardest hit by the war (in the east around Vucovar).

Croatia was the most economically successful region in Tito's Yugoslavia, with a thriving tourist industry supporting manufacturing, engineering and service industries. Today, tourism is once again a major foreign-currency earner, but heavy industry has suffered since the late 1980s and there is still a problem with unemployment, which stands at almost 18 per cent (2004 figures). Domestically the government must fight unemployment whilst maintaining proper fiscal controls (inflation has steadied at around 2–3 per cent, which is a good platform for further progress). Several initiatives and ministries have been created to restart domestic small businesses, whilst Croatia must also privatise

Politics

major industries, trying hard to avoid the disasters of neighbouring ex-communist peers.

The undisputed and overall aim of the government is the gradual integration of Croatia back into the world economy, and to achieve EU accession. The government has worked hard to reform several key governmental processes in preparation for joining the EU and to formalise relations and connections with the IMF, WYO and other regional and world organisations. Croatia has done relatively well in terms of foreign investment, coming third in terms of dollar investment per head of population in a list of 'emerging' European nations.

Parliamentary democracy

Croatia's constitution was adopted in December 1990 after a free election in the spring of that year, but the original two-chamber parliament was changed to a one-chamber legislature in 2001. Suffrage is from the age of 16 if the individual is economically active, and universal from the age of 18. The president, elected by popular vote, serves a term of five years. He or she acts as the country's representative, but the main power rests with the legislative body. Presidential power is limited to two terms. The prime minister is then chosen by the president, the appointee taking into account the balance of power in parliament.

The heart of Croatian governance, Sv Marko in Zagreb

The government consists of the prime minister, one or more deputies, plus a Council of Ministers chosen by the prime minister and approved by the parliament. The government acts as the catalyst for legislative changes and forward planning.

The Sabor is the single-chamber parliament or legislature, having no less than 100 members and no more than 160 members (currently 152). Members are elected for four years. A multi-party system, with pre-designated balances within the Sabor, ensures coalition governments. The Sabor then elects the judicial arm of government. Judges serve an eight-year term.

Franjo Tuđman – 'father' of the Croatian Democratic Republic

One man stands out as the leading light throughout the troubled birth of modern Croatia. Franjo Tuđman was the voice of the Croat freedom movement. He became its first president, wielding an immense amount of power. Born in Veliko Trgovisce in northern Croatia in 1922, Tuđman took to politics at an early age. In 1940 he was imprisoned for his membership of the national democratic movement, after which he became staunchly anti-Fascist. After World War II he was employed in the Ministry of Defence and on the army general staff.

Pugari guards keep watch at Varaždin

He reached the rank of general but his nationalist feelings were growing; he left military service in 1961 because he saw the army being increasingly dominated by Serbs.

During the 1960s, he established the Institute for the History of the Labour Movement, received a doctorate in Political Science, worked as a lecturer at the university and was also a Yugoslav parliamentary representative from 1965–9. Publication of several academic texts led to his membership of the Croatian Academy of Sciences and Arts in 1970. He was expelled from the communist party in 1967 because of his ultra-nationalist opinions, and imprisoned in 1971 during the 'Croatian Spring'. Instigated by a document on the Croatian language by Croatian poets and linguists, this became a much wider civil rights movement that demanded more freedom for Croatia. Tito countered it with mass arrests, and more than 2,000 people were imprisoned.

In February 1981 Tuđman was sentenced to three years' imprisonment for his 'anti-Yugoslav' attitude, and banned from speaking to foreign journalists. However, in 1987 his passport was returned to him and he travelled extensively, giving lectures to expatriate Croat communities and others, drumming up support for an independent Croatia.

In 1989 he established the Croatian Democratic Union (HDZ). The party won the first free elections in 1990, and Tuđman was elected president. He refused to recognise Serb rights within Croatia, and this brought the country into conflict with its neighbour Serbia. During the conflict Tuđman used his military experience to organise the Croatian Army; he successfully halted the Serbs, beating their army at Krajina in 1995.

Tuđman remained immensely popular at home, winning presidential elections in 1992 and 1997. However, he became increasingly autocratic. Newspapers were closed down and influence became centralised in the hands of a small group of confidants and family members. He fell ill with stomach cancer, and died in Zagreb in December 1999 while still in power.

Current 'movers and shakers'

The current Croatian president is Stjepan Mesić (elected for a further five-year term in 2005). He was born in December 1934, and graduated from law school in Zagreb. A prominent student leader, he was jailed for his part in the Spring Uprising of 1971. In 1990 he became secretary of the HDZ and Croatia's first prime minister. He resigned from the HDZ in 1994, setting up his own party, the Croatian Independent Democrats (HND). In 1997 Mesić and some of the HND joined the Croatian People's Party (NHS). He was elected president after Tuđman's death.

Elections in November 2003 saw Dr Ivo Sanader appointed prime minister. He is head of the Croatian Democratic Union party and was an aide to Tuđman.

Culture

Croatian culture is a complex web woven of many strands. Much of it derives from the influences of its many different colonial overlords. Styles and fashions in art, music and architecture arrived here from all around the known world; conversely, only a few native Croatian influences or individuals have reached a global audience.

Today, though, as an independent country, Croatia can foster and promote its domestic talent in all fields without having to wrap successes in a Yugoslav banner. This should allow future talent the freedom and the confidence to blossom.

ARCHITECTURE

The architecture in Croatia is incredibly varied, given its small landmass. Unfortunately there have been some losses during the recent war. Dubrovnik was badly damaged in 1991, though with the aid of international funds it has been rebuilt to a very high standard. However, there remain important but less high-profile buildings and historic quarters in the eastern region that still await help to bring them back to their pre-war state.

Ancient architecture

The country abounds in exceptional ancient sites. Illyrian fortresses were crude affairs, but many continued to be useful for centuries. The foundations of many of the fortified villages just inland from the coast were also built by Illyrians. The amphitheatre at Pula and Diocletian's Palace at Split are supreme examples of grand Roman architecture. Less dramatic but larger sites such as the one at Salona and the artefacts of the Aquae Balissae spa towns in eastern Croatia show that the Romans were well established and living a luxurious life here during the early centuries of the first millennium.

Romanesque

The decline and fall of Rome and the rise of Constantinople (the Byzantine empire) brought a flurry of architecture, both religious – the Romanesque style – and civil. Romanesque architecture is characterised by simple rounded arches and vaulted ceilings, perhaps best seen in the 6th-century Basilica of

Euphasius at Poreč, or the later Cathedral of St Mary the Great on Rab and the Church of St Donat in Zadar. It often mimicked Roman forms, sometimes using Roman stone from abandoned Roman sites.

Gothic and Renaissance

When the Venetians took the Dalmatian coast, they brought with them the more ornate Gothic style. This was typified by the pointed rather than rounded arch. The numerous buildings they erected on the islands and the main coastline were often refurbished and updated as styles changed, so finding pure Gothic architecture is difficult. Try the Cathedral of St Mark on Korčula, the Rector's Palace in Dubrovnik or Kamerlango Tower in Trogir.

More buildings display the Renaissance lines of the 15th and 16th centuries. This was the time when Venetian power was at its height. City walls such as those at Trogir indicate their prowess in techniques of fortification, while exceptional civic buildings can be found in just about every port on every Dalmatian island. Look particularly for the Old Loggia at Šibenik and the town halls at Trogir and Split.

Baroque

During the Ottoman period (1526–1693), walls of fortresses across the country were enhanced, but little else remains of Ottoman influence because mosques and *madrasas* (Islamic religious schools, often found in the grounds of a mosque) were destroyed

The elegant neo-classical Croatian National Theatre in Zagreb

Croatian costumes

Modernist

In the modernist era (post-1750), fashion sought inspiration from the past, and both neo-Gothic and neo-classical styles are well represented. The finest ensemble has to be the 'green horseshoe' of fine squares set out in Donji Grad, Zagreb, in the late 19th century. Other examples include the Parliament Building, also in Zagreb, and the Church of Saints Peter and Paul at Osijek.

THE ARTS

The influence of foreign-born artists and artisans is a predominant feature of the Croatian arts, be they painters and sculptors from Rome, Venice, Constantinople or Vienna. However, a few domestic luminaries have also graced the scene.

Sculptors

Much of Croatia's finest sculpture has a religious theme, with churches and monasteries being the major beneficiaries. However, most of the men who laboured, often for a lifetime, on these projects, remain anonymous.

One of the highlights of the northern Dalmatia coast is the intricate stone portal of Trogir cathedral. Master Radovan's signature lays claim to the work, but though he is thought to be a local mason, nothing is known of the man or his life.

Woodworker Master Buvina carved the doorway of the cathedral in Split in the early 13th century, the 28 panels

in the wake of their withdrawal. What followed in northern Croatia was the arrival of the Baroque architecture fashionable throughout the Habsburg empire at the time (late 16th to mid-18th century).

Baroque is characterised by flowing lines and movement and marks a departure from (rather than a development of) the structured forms of Renaissance buildings. Churches became highly ornamented, while civic buildings and palaces assumed enormous proportions.

Zagreb is home to many fine Baroque edifices, including the Museum of Croatian History, Vojković-Oršić Palace. Elsewhere it can be seen at its best at the Cathedral of the Assumption in Varaždin or the façades of the main square in Požega.

being considered a masterpiece of the Romanesque period.

A little more is known about Giorgio Orsini or Jurij Dalmatinac (1420–73), the master mason who worked on Šibenik cathedral. He became one of the Italian Renaissance's finest architects.

The most renowned modern Croatian artist was the sculptor Ivan Meštrović (1883–1962), who was from a humble background but whose talent was recognised from an early age. He broke onto the international scene after winning the Rome Internationale award in 1911. Politically active after World War I, he set up a committee aimed at creating a Slavic nation. His most productive artistic era was between the wars. After World War II he left Yugoslavia to escape Communism. He settled in the US, but left a large body of work in his homeland. The best collection is at the museum in Zagreb that was one of his homes.

Artists

Croatia has seen two major domestic artistic movements that have achieved international acclaim. In Dubrovnik during the 15th and 16th centuries, the wealth of artistic talent, coupled with the support of rich benefactors, led to the creation of what is now called the 'Dubrovnik School', a loose affiliation of individuals and their pupils who worked mainly on religious buildings. Though not of the school, the Croatian artist Julije Klovic (1498–1578) was regarded

as the best miniaturist of his era, though he did little work in his native land.

Much later, in the 1930s, the Hlebinska slikarska škola (Hlebine School), centred on the village of Hlebine near Zagreb, appeared on the world stage. The school developed a social movement called *Zemlja* (Land), and was particularly devoted to peasant, or so-called naïve, art. Principal members included Krsto Hegedusi, Ivan Generalic, Franjo Mraz and Mirko Virius, and their work is best seen at the Museum of Primitive Art in Zagreb.

Today the Museum of Modern and Contemporary Art in Rijeka showcases a selection of the best of Croatian and Slovenian artists in temporary exhibitions, though these artists have yet to find a worldwide audience. Miroslav Šutej (b.1936) is perhaps the best known. He designed the Croatian national flag and coat of arms.

Bishop Grgur Ninski, by Meštrović

Marshal Tito and the communists

'Father' of communist Yugoslavia, its creator and guiding hand, Tito was born Josip Broz in May 1892 in the village of Kumrovec – then part of the Austro-Hungarian empire, now on the northeastern border of Croatia. He was one of a vast family of 15 born to his Roman Catholic peasant-farmer parents.

Young Josip left school at the age of 12 to become a locksmith but, after completing his apprenticeship, he decided to leave home, travelling extensively throughout Europe. On his return at the age of 18 he joined the Croatian Social Democratic Party. A military conscript, he was sent to the Russian front at the outbreak of World War I and spent two years as a prisoner of war. On his release in

Tito's humble birthplace at Kumrovec

1917 he joined the Russian Bolsheviks, fighting with Lenin's Red Guards in the civil war that preceded the communist victory. Now imbued with the spirit of Bolshevism, he returned to his homeland in 1920 and joined the communist Party.

In 1927 he became a member of the Zagreb cell of the communist Party, and so began his meteoric ascendancy through the party system. In 1934, after being arrested yet again, he was named a full member of the party Politburo and Central Committee, taking the name Tito as a *nom de guerre*. In 1935 he visited the Soviet Union as a Balkans representative on the central Comintern (the international pan-communist committee), and finally in 1940 he was officially named as the head of Yugoslavia's communist Party.

Tito waited until the Soviet Union entered World War II before organising military resistance to the Nazi invaders of Yugoslavia. The underground political cells that had been formed when the communist Party had been outlawed proved a very effective foundation from which to mount guerrilla operations throughout the region, but another group of freedom fighters also felt themselves to be Yugoslavia's legitimate resistance movement – the mainly Serbian Chetniks. As the war progressed, Allied support favoured Tito and his partisans, who in 1943 were recognised as the official opposition during the Tehran Conference, when the leaders of the Allies (Churchill, Roosevelt and Stalin) met to discuss a strategy for the defeat of the Axis. Having formed revolutionary governments in areas of the country freed from Axis control, Tito was in an excellent position to consolidate his power base when the country was finally completely free. He systematically purged the country of opposition and Yugoslavia became a communist state.

Tito in his military uniform

Tito took federal Yugoslavia on an independent path, incurring Stalin's wrath when he also courted the West in order to get financial aid. In 1948 Yugoslavia was expelled from the Cominform (a pan-communist organisation founded in the late 1940s that was an arena for the exchange of policy and general information). This effectively cut it off from the Soviet camp. And although after Stalin's death Tito signed an accord, the Belgrade Declaration (1955), with Soviet successor Nikita Khrushchev, he continued to move beyond the hardline communist doctrine, treading what he called a 'third way', aligned neither to the Soviet bloc nor to the West. Tito worked tirelessly to promote this alternative policy; by the 1970s this had resulted in a loose affiliation of 25 countries.

At home Tito had no obvious successor, and he strove to create a balance, establishing six republics and two autonomous regions with limited but real powers. Some have maintained that this set republics against one another, fostering resentments that fuelled the conflicts of the 1990s.

Tito was made 'president for life' in 1974. He died of cancer on 4 May 1980 at the ripe old age of 88.

Festivals

Croatia has some excellent events, with world-acclaimed celebrations of performing arts sitting side by side with age-old traditional festivities – including celebrations of military victories, reverential religious processions and harvest festivals for crops from grape to grain. The range on offer is very wide, reflecting the diverse lifestyles of the Croatian people.

The following is a list of the major festivals and events that take place each year around the country.

January
Children's Piano Festival, *Osijek*
Snow Queen Trophy, *Sljeme Zagreb (FIS ski event)*

February
Carnival of the Riviera, *Opatija*
Feast of St Blaise, *Dubrovnik (town saint's day, 3 February)*
Lastovo Festival
Shrovetide Sezona, *Kraljevica (masked ball, Shrove Tuesday)*

March
Easter processions, *Korčula*

April
St Mark's Festival, *Zagreb (second half of April)*
St Vincent's Day, *Korčula (commemoration of an ancient battle with the Kumpanjija dance, 28 April)*

May
Festival of Tambour Music, *Osijek (with traditional instruments, mid-May)*
Josip Štolcer Slavanski Memorial Festival, *Čakovec (dedicated to the Croatian composer; first half of May)*
Puppet Theatre Festival, *Osijek (early May)*
Rab Tournament *(with medieval costumed parade, 9 May)*
Small Theatre Festival, *Rijeka (first half of May)*

June
Brodsko Kolo Folklore Festival, *Slavonski Brod (mid-June)*
Dance Week, *Zagreb (featuring all styles of dance, first week in June)*
International Children's Festival, *Šibenik (music, dance and theatre, last week in June and first in July)*
Klapa Festival, *Omiš (featuring traditional folk music, all month to early July)*
Satire Days, *Zagreb (all month)*

Sonnet Day of Hanibal Lucič, *Hvar (festival dedicated to local poet with readings)*
Summer Festival, *Hvar (traditional music, dance and theatre, all summer)*

July
Classical Summer, *Labin (classical and folk performances, July and August)*
Đakovacki Vezovi, *Đakova (folkloric festival, first week in July)*
Dubrovnik Summer Festival *(the largest in Croatia, mid-July to end August)*
Histria Festival, *Pula (opera, theatre and musical performances, July to mid-August)*
International Folklore Festival, *Zagreb (end July)*
Krk Summer Festival *(folkloric and mainstream arts performances, mid-July to end August)*
Margaretina, *Omis (feast day of St Margaret, 13 July)*
Music Festival, *Zadar (instrumental music, all month and early August)*
Music Festival, *Osor (chamber music, mid-July to mid-August)*
Pag Carnival *(31 July)*
St Theodore's Day, *Korčula (celebrated by the Moreška dance, commemorating a battle between Christian and Muslim forces, 29 July)*
Tournament of Rab *(re-run of the May tournament, 25–27 July)*

August
Baljanska Noć, *Bale (traditional fair and celebrations, first Sunday in August)*

Festival of Bumbari, *Vodnjan (a unique donkey race plus other folklore activities)*
Festival of Puppet Theatre, *Zagreb (end August to early September)*
Olympics of Ancient Sports, *Brođanci*
St Roch's Day, *Postrana, Korčula Island (with the Mostra traditional sword dance, 16 August)*
Sinjska Alka, *Sinj (traditional festival celebrating the ousting of the Turks, early August)*
Summer Festival, *Novi Vinodolski (mid-month)*
Trka na Prstenac (Tilting at the Ring), *Barban (a traditional jousting tournament)*

September
Grape Festival, *Buje (wine tasting, parades and concerts, last weekend in September)*
Vinkovačke Jeseni *(the Vinkovci festival of folk music and dance, September and October)*

October
Bela Nedeja, *Kastav (wine festival, first Sunday in October)*
Marunada, *Lovran (chestnut festival, mid-October)*

November
International Music Festival, *Pula (first half of November)*

December
Osijek Town Day *(2 December)*

The Venetian Republic

The influence of Venice is evident throughout this region. But just how did a city built on a lagoon and without any firm territory become a leading power in the early second millennium?

Venice's rise began after it moved to the most sheltered sector of the lagoon, around the Rivo Alto or Ri-Alto ('high bank'), to escape the forces of the Carolingian ruler Pepin in 810. It had been a republic since 697, and slowly began to reap the rewards of shipbuilding expertise, good management and canny business dealings, preferring diplomacy to destruction, agreement to aggression. In the latter half of the 12th century, Marco Polo's journey to China opened up trading with the Far East, giving Venice the monopoly on trade in luxury goods such as silk.

Obviously they built a network of allies, but they also had enemies. The Slav pirates attacking from the coast of Dalmatia were a thorn in their side that needed removing. It was typical of their style that they not only paid the Dalmatians a yearly fee for safe passage through their waters to the Mediterranean, but that the Doge also set about building diplomatic bridges with the Dalmatians' Slav neighbours. In the year 1000 the Venetian fleet sought a final showdown with the pirates. Venice took control of the Dalmatian coast, its first major territorial acquisition, forcing Dalmatian cities to pay tribute to it rather than the other way round.

The Fourth Crusade, in 1204, proved a blessing for Venice. This time the army was not going to march from the west to Jerusalem, but sail

The lion, symbol of the Venetian Republic

Venetian port buildings on the Adriatic

Venice became the most influential power in the Mediterranean, further humiliating Byzantines by incorporating the plundered treasures of Constantinople into their grand new status symbol, St Mark's Square. For the next 250 years, all Venetian dominions, including the Dalmatian coast, benefited, as fine port towns were created and trade kept public and private coffers full.

Venice's decline began in the mid-15th century, with the rise of Ottoman power in the eastern Mediterranean. Venetian trade routes were blocked. At around the same time Vasco da Gama heralded the end of the Venetian monopoly of trade with the Far East when he rounded the Cape of Good Hope in 1497. Spain, Portugal and the Netherlands could now trade with the Far East without encroaching on Venetian waters.

In 1508, an alliance of France, Spain and papal forces attacked the city, taking many riches and appropriating territory. However, the final nail in the coffin of the Venetian Republic came in 1797, when Napoleon annexed what was left. After Napoleon's demise, Venice was taken by Austria, becoming a pawn in greater European power struggles until it joined the new country of Italy in 1866.

across the Mediterranean to Egypt to attack the Saracen forces from the southwest. Only Venice had the resources and expertise to fund and build a fleet sufficiently large to carry the Christian troops. Leaders of the crusade commissioned ships; Venice offered to loan them 50 more in return for half the booty and land captured during the campaign.

The crusade ended ignominiously in the sacking of Constantinople. Constantinople had been seen as impenetrable; the subsequent loss of esteem and of wealth brought about a change in attitude by the Byzantines themselves, and their enemies.

First steps

Set in the northeastern corner of the Balkan peninsula, where it meets the top of the Italian peninsula, Croatia's boundary in the west is the Adriatic Sea. The countries on its land boundaries are still in a state of flux from the dismantling of communist Yugoslavia. In the north lie Slovenia and Hungary, while in the east and south are Serbia, Bosnia-Herzegovina and Montenegro, whose boundaries with Croatia are internationally recognised but whose borders with each other may yet change again.

WHEN TO GO

With so many fascinating stone and brick monuments and buildings to visit, it really doesn't matter what time of year you visit Croatia. Every season brings something special to the country. Depending on the time of year, different colours play on façades, and smells of harvests or seasonal foods fill the air.

Summer

Glorious blue skies and daytime temperatures in the upper 20°s C (low 80°s F), hours of sunshine and warm evenings draw thousands of visitors in the summer. The island ferries busy themselves between the Adriatic islands, arts festivals are in full swing, and the waters are at their warmest for swimming or diving. Of course the downside of a peak-season visit is the sheer number of fellow travellers, which in turn puts pressure on the infrastructure. Roads, cafés, marinas,

hotels and campsites will be at their busiest, and prices rise too; it may also be a little too hot for any strenuous activity such as hiking or cycling.

Autumn

The crowds depart by the middle of September, making churches and museums – as well as the narrow alleys of the old towns – easier to explore. There are seats in the fashionable cafés once again, and ferries and roads are less congested. Temperatures drop a little, which is great for outdoor sports and activities, and the sun's warm glow is better for photographers than the harsh high summer light. It's harvest time for vines, fruit and maize, and somnolent villages now wake to a flurry of activity. Migratory birds stop off on the long journey south.

But a late visit has some downsides. Ferries run less frequently in mid-September, and even less often in early October, making island-hopping, or day visits from the mainland, more difficult. In turn, island museums reduce their opening hours, or close altogether except to pre-booked groups. The weather becomes less dependable, particularly in Istria and Kvarner – so take a sweater for those cooler evenings, and rainwear for the odd thunderstorm.

Winter

A winter wonderland awaits those who want to visit between November and March, as much of the interior of Croatia gets a good covering of snow. Zagreb dons its winter coat as the gas lamps of the old town glow against the white flakes. Street life goes on throughout the season, though: Croatians are used to the cold. The islands don't always see snow, but they do hunker down against the storms that can play across the Adriatic, and against the fierce cold that the bora brings in winter. Many bars and restaurants close completely at the end of October, or move their tables and chairs inside – not the best environment for non-smokers (*see Smoking, p35*).

Spring

Temperatures start rising, and the hours of sunlight increase. The birds return, heading north this time. The leaves on trees and budding crops signal another fertile year ahead. Outside the waterfront cafés and restaurants, canopies and umbrellas rise

like mushrooms, signalling it's time for business once again. The bora warms a touch, but can still inflict a nasty sting if the temperature drops.

WHERE TO GO

The Dalmatian coast with its offshore archipelagos makes the perfect place for relaxed island-hopping, with excellent waters for snorkelling and diving and beaches for sun-worshippers. Dubrovnik is outstanding, but it's only one of more than a dozen incredible fortified towns scattered across the region. Choose Paklenica National Park for hiking or climbing, or take to two wheels for excellent cycling throughout the region.

Like Dalmatia, Istria is replete with Italianate architecture, but also secretes

The verdant Zagorje

a string of tiny hilltop villages that are just waiting to be explored. For grand 19th-century resorts head to the Opatija Riviera in Kvarner, where the Habsburg princes used to play.

The capital, Zagreb, is a likeable city, still operating at a people-friendly level. Its architecture and its café life make it a great 'city break' destination.

Continental Croatia doesn't have the dramatic landscapes of the coast, but its onion-domed churches and estuarine natural habitats offer sightseeing pleasures away from the masses. The traditional lifestyle of the east continues to flourish, centred on the seasonal activities of the farm.

Croatia is a compact country that offers something remarkable in every region – whether it be fantastic Baroque churches, Renaissance palaces, mineral springs or national parks. You could easily combine some or all of these into a two-week holiday, or spend longer and savour your favourites.

WHAT TO WEAR

Layering is the key here. In summer light cotton or breathable clothing is advisable for sightseeing. It might be wise to carry a warm layer (a fleece is ideal) for the occasional evening breeze. Be aware that swimsuits and bikinis are not suitable attire for the towns and should be confined to the beaches, where of course it's also quite acceptable to wear nothing at all!

Spring and autumn will generally be warm, so keep to light cotton outfits, but pack a couple of warmer layers for the fresher evenings, and one cold-weather option too. In the winter months, warm and waterproof clothing and stout footwear are a must throughout the country.

It is still wise to wear, or carry with you, items of clothing that will cover your thighs and shoulders if you intend to visit churches and monasteries. Remember these are spiritual places to those who worship here.

Café society is an important part of life here

GETTING AROUND

Until the latter decades of the 20th century, water played a much more important role than land in transportation for the Istrians and Dalmatians. Ferry services are still the lifeblood of the island communities, and provide an excellent way to tour the coast.

A satisfactory road network links all communities, but the long, sinuous Jadranska Magistrala highway, hugging the Dalmatian coast, becomes clogged with traffic in summer. It consists of a dangerous series of switchbacks that claims lives every year. The motorway system is developing, allowing quicker routes. Latest estimates put the completion of the last section from Split to Dubrovnik at 2009: the lack of suitable ground on which to build it has made this project a real engineering challenge.

Croatia's railway network doesn't venture to western Istria or south of Split, but could be useful for touring the heart of the country. Rolling stock isn't always new, however, and trains can be slow due to the many level crossings along the routes.

All major towns and a number of islands have airports, with services linked to the air hub in Zagreb – but rarely to other Croatian airports. It's an efficient way of reaching one's destination, but it isn't a suitable way of touring.

FORMALITIES

You must register with the police within 48 hours of arrival in Croatia, but if you are booked into a hotel they should do it for you. If you stay in a private room or apartment, ask about the procedure.

All tourists (including Croatians staying away from their place of permanent residence) must pay a daily tourist tax. This even applies to those staying in private homes, with relatives, or on boats and campsites.

The road network is generally good

Children aged 12 to 18 pay 50 per cent of the adult rate, while children under 12, handicapped travellers, or those undergoing medical treatment are exempt.

CULTURE SHOCK

The Croatians are a warm and friendly people, and you will certainly be made to feel very much at home during your visit. But here are a few non-scientific pointers to the curiosities you may encounter on your trip.

Say what?

As you travel around the country you'll realise that there are several distinct accents or dialects, as one would imagine in a country that has undergone such diverse historical development. For example, in Istria 'two' is *dve*, whereas in Zagreb and the east it's *dva*. For foreign visitors, it's really just a matter of realising that the phrase you painstakingly perfected in the café in Dubrovnik won't necessarily be understood in the café in Osijek.

The *bora*

The *bora*, a fierce wind that blows from the north down the Adriatic, has had a great influence on the life of Dalmatians and Istrians. Many island towns are set in the lee of hills to curb

Windows onto the world at this piazza apartment

its sting, and crops and livestock are raised within sturdy stone stockades to protect them from its worst effects.

Yet without the *bora*, life would be very different. It provides the cool arid breeze needed for the drying of the Dalmatian *pšut* (ham), and the air movement needed for the pollination of olives, fruits and vines.

The *bora* is unusual in that it generally blows at night and in the mornings, but by midday has died down to a gentle zephyr, leaving the afternoons calm.

Home brew

If you stay in self-catering accommodation, in rented rooms, or on small, family-run campsites, it won't be long before you are offered home-made *rakia* (a spirit distilled from the grape skins after they have been pressed for wine). You'll also see it sold at roadside stalls in Istria and along the Dalmatian coast. It's extremely palatable – but watch out! It's very strong and can give you a huge hangover.

Tread carefully

Most beaches in Croatia are pebble or shingle, not sand, and where there is no beach a concrete lido often provides access for swimming and a place to sunbathe. These environments are hard on the feet, so it's worth investing in a pair of beach shoes or sandals. These are sold in resorts and island towns.

Postcards showcase the best of Croatia

Smoking

Croatia is a country of smokers, and there's little concern shown for non-smokers in restaurants and bars. However, during the summer this doesn't cause much of a problem, as people can eat and drink alfresco.

To answer your question

Unofficial tourist offices abound, usually signposted with INFO or TOURIST INFO. These are not necessarily bad agencies, but they may exist to promote certain boat trips or rooms and they won't have the excellent Croatian government-issued information. The addresses we have included under each location are the official tourist information offices.

Zagreb

A new capital but an old city, Zagreb in many ways epitomises Croatia. It is energetic, vibrant and forward-looking, yet has pride in its history and traditions. It has only been a capital city since 1991, when Croatia declared independence, but it played an important role within the Habsburg and Austro-Hungarian empires for many centuries, and has long had the cultural trimmings (theatre, museums and so on) that befit a major city. It stages several major arts festivals throughout the year.

Zagreb developed as two contrasting towns late in the first millennium. Kaptol – on one hill – was the bishopric, while Gradec – on an adjacent hill – was the supporting secular settlement. Gradec became a free city under King Bela IV in 1242, and increased in influence when chosen as the seat for the Ban (the governor of Croatia under the empire) and the regional Croatian parliament. The two towns were never particularly friendly, seeing each other as rivals rather than allies; however, the devastating earthquake of 1880 brought irrevocable changes, when much of the city had to be rebuilt. A new Zagreb rose from the desolation. Gradec and Kaptol were unified, their fortifications dismantled and a 'modern' city built outside their respective walls.

Today the city centre consists of the two medieval settlements, now collectively known as Gornji Grad (Upper Town), and Donji Grad (Lower Town), which developed in the wake of the earthquake. Trg bana Jelačić (bana Jelačić Square) ties the two elements together. It's one of the liveliest of Zagreb's many squares, and plays host to the main city tourist office. A short funicular links the two sections of the downtown area, but it's not a long climb for the averagely fit.

GORNJI GRAD

The religious and political heart of Croatia throughout its long and complicated history, Gornji Grad still

Relaxing in Trg bana Jelačić

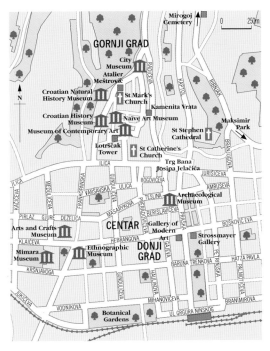

modern studio. Today it houses an impressive collection of his work in bronze, wood and stone, and includes design sketches used in preparation for various works. The gardens are used as an open-air gallery.

The Meštrović Foundation, which manages the museum and another in Split (*see p86*), is also the custodian of Meštrović's personal papers, which are available for professional artists and academics to study.

Mletačka 8. Tel: (01) 485 1123. Open: Tue–Fri 10am–6pm, Sat & Sun 10am–2pm. Admission fee.

plays host to the modern trappings of church and state, including the Bishop's Palace (now the Ban's Palace) and the Sabor (Parliament Building), built in 1910 (neither open to the public). Many of the medieval buildings were lost in the 1880 earthquake, but Gornji Grad still has an 'olde worlde' atmosphere, helped in the evening by the glow of its gas streetlights.

Atelier Meštrović (Ivan Meštrović Studio)

One of the world's leading figures in the genre of sculpture during the 20th century, Meštrović (*see p23*) bought this 17th-century house in the early 1920s and turned it into a

Hrvatski muzej Naivne Umjetnosti (Croatian Museum of Naïve Art)

Croatian artists have been the leading lights in this genre, so it is fitting that a museum has been dedicated to their work. The 'peasant' style, as it is sometimes called, is characterised by bright colours and strong images – usually of country themes – with little regard for perspective. The Hlebine School (*see p23*) is known internationally and is well represented here, though there are pieces by artists from all across the country.

Čirilometodska 3. Tel: (01) 485 1911;
www.hmnu.org. Open: Tue–Fri
10am–6pm, Sat & Sun 10am–1pm.
Admission fee.

Hrvatski Povijesni muzej (Croatian History Museum)

The convoluted history of Croatia is well documented through the galleries of the splendid Baroque Vojković-Oršić Palace. The fancy military uniforms and flurry of heraldic pennants hark back to the post-Ottoman glory days, while paintings and documents bring to life key events.

Matoševa 9. Tel: (01) 485 1900;
www.hismus.hr. Open: Mon–Fri
10am–5pm, Sat & Sun 10am–1pm.
Admission fee.

Hrvatski Prirodoslovni muzej (Croatian Natural History Museum)

Housed in the 18th-century Amadeo Palace, this vast collection runs the whole gamut, from how the earth was formed (with examples of rock formations and precious and semi-precious minerals), to a stuffed animal collection that highlights the many creatures that still roam the national parks around the country – though you are very unlikely to see them in the wild. The palaeontology collection is particularly fine, but its most important find, the skull of Krapina Man, a Neanderthal specimen found in a village in northern Croatia (*see p129*), is not on public show.

Demetrova 1. Tel: (01) 485 1700;
www.hpm.hr. Open: Tue–Fri 10am–5pm,
Sat & Sun 10am–1pm. Admission fee.

Kamenita vrata (Stone Gate)

The last remaining gate into the old town of Gradec, Stone Gate is in fact relatively young – it was finished in 1760. Within the gate, on the left as you enter from Kaptol, is a small chapel dedicated to the miraculous painting, *Madonna and Child*, which was the only part of the previous wooden gate to survive a rampaging fire in 1731. It is still the object of much reverence from today's city dwellers.

Katedrala Marijina Uznesenja (Cathedral of the Assumption of the Virgin Mary, though also dedicated to St Stephen and St Ladislas)

The exceptional spires of St Stephen's, the city's most important centre of religious worship, pierce the skies above Gornji Grad like rapiers. This outstanding church has 11th-century antecedents. It has been destroyed and rebuilt many times during its long history, but retains its medieval footprint.

The current façade with the spires is neo-Gothic, designed by Friedrich von Schmidt and Herman Bollé after the 1880 earthquake. The large arched doorway and rose window hark back directly to earlier examples in Šibenik or Zadar, but appear here on a grander scale. The interior has been redecorated

many times, and several altars were designed by Bollé during the 1880s renovations. Look specifically for a triptych in the sacristy by Albrecht Dürer (1495), *Relief of the Blessed Alojzije Stepinac* by Ivan Meštrović, and for tombs such as those of Krsto Frankopan and Petar Zrinski, martyrs to the cause of Croatian independence in 1671.
Kaptol. Tel: (01) 481 4727. Open: daily 8am–8pm.

Kula Lotrščak (Lotrščak Tower)

In the 13th century, Lotrščak Tower was an essential part of Gradec's fortifications. Today it offers panoramic views over the city from its small dome; it is also home to the gun that has been fired every day at noon – with a few exceptions – since 1877. The gun was originally used to synchronise the peal of all the church bells in the city as they called the faithful to midday Mass.
Strossmayerovo Šetalište. Tel: (01) 485 1768. Open: Tue–Sun 11am–8pm. Admission fee.

A medieval atmosphere prevails in Gornji Grad

Muzej Grada Zagreba (City Museum)

The city museum charts the history of Zagreb from the prehistoric era to modern times. It includes fascinating paintings and drawings of Gradec and Kaptol before the earthquake, and shows how the late 19th-century town and the 20th-century urban landscape were planned and developed.
Opatička 20. Tel: (01) 485 1361;
www.mdc.hr/mgz. Open: Tue–Fri 10am–6pm, Sat & Sun 10am–1pm. Admission fee.

Muzej Suvreneme Umjetnosti (Museum of Contemporary Art)

As with the Gallery of Modern Art (*see p43*), the narrow focus of this museum, devoted solely to 19th- and 20th-century Croatian artists, may mean that it's for art lovers only.

However, its strength in depth makes it important for lovers of Modernism. *Katarinin trg 2. Tel: (01) 485 1808; www.mdc.hr/msu. Open: Tue–Sat 11am–7pm, Sun 10am–1pm. Admission fee. Free on Tue.*

Sv Katarina (St Catherine's Church)

The finest Baroque church in Zagreb, St Catherine's presents a restrained and demure façade yet offers a delicious riot

Sv Marko is famed for its ornate roof

of decoration within. Ornate stucco covers all the surfaces not offering a side altar or ceiling fresco, while at the end of the nave behind the main altar is an impressive monumental wall mural, *St Catherine amongst the Alexandrian Philosophers* by Kristof Jelovšek. *Katarinski trg. Tel: (01) 485 1950. Open: daily 10am–1pm.*

Sv Marko (St Mark's Church)

One of the most celebrated churches in Croatia for its colourful roof tiles depicting the coats of arms of the kingdoms of Croatia, Dalmatia and Slavonia, and the city of Zagreb, St Mark's used to act as the parish church for Gradec. It dates from the 13th century, though has undergone many alterations, but the original Gothic doorway (currently under renovation and not *in situ*) is a fine example of its kind, with the rising arch decorated with statues of Jesus, Mary and St Mark flanked by the 12 Apostles. Inside the church you'll find modern decoration, including a collection of pieces by Meštrović and some interesting frescoes depicting Croat royalty. Flanking the church are the Parliament Building and the Bansko dvori (Ban's Palace), the seat of the Croatian governors during Hungarian and Austro-Hungarian rule. *Markov Trg. Tel: (01) 485 1611. Open: daily 11am–4pm & 5.30–7pm.*

DONJI GRAD

One of the finest examples of late 19th-century town planning in Europe,

Donji Grad clearly bears the hallmark of architect Herman Bollé. Much of Donji Grad boasts wide avenues flanked by neo-classical façades; these are dotted with many public squares, now overflowing with busy cafés. A series of large squares and gardens, designed by urban planner Milan Lenucci and now known as the 'green horseshoe', is home to some of the city's most important museums and monumental sculpture. They give Donji Grad a very airy feel, helped by the recent cleaning of sooty office and apartment buildings.

Arheološki muzej (Archaeological Museum)

A comprehensive collection of artefacts chronicles the early history of what is now Croatia. The pre-Classical Age displays include the famed Vučedol Dove, found in the east. Finely crafted by an ancient tribe, this three-legged vessel is witness to the sophistication of early humankind. Other finds include the longest extant Etruscan text, used to bandage a mummy found in the region of Zagreb. The Greek and Roman sections have high-quality items, many found at the Roman city of Salona in northern Dalmatia (*see pp79–80*), while the later collections concentrate on the birth of the first Croatia – the short-lived 'land of the Princes'. The museum's numismatic collection is reputedly the largest in Europe, with examples dating back to Celtic times. *Trg N Zrinskog 19. Tel: (01) 487 3101;*

www.amz.hr. Open: Tue–Fri 10am–5pm, Sat & Sun 10am–1pm. Admission fee.

Botanički Vrt (Botanical Gardens)

Founded in 1889 as a means to develop the new science of botany, the gardens now contain over 10,000 species of plants from around the world set in around 5 hectares (12,350 acres). The two ponds with their water lilies and bridges make a particularly pleasant vista in the middle of the city, but it is the shade of the mature trees that offers a delightful contrast to the more open squares of the 'green horseshoe'. *Marulićev trg 9. Tel: (01) 484 4002. Open: Apr–May & Oct Mon–Tue 9am–2.30pm, Wed–Sun 9am–6pm; June–Sept Mon–Tue 9am–2.30pm, Wed–Sun 9am–7pm. Free. Guided tours: admission fee.*

Etnografski muzej (Ethnographic Museum)

The rich tapestry of traditional life in Croatia is showcased here, with a vast collection of 60,000 items, including folk handicrafts such as embroidery and lace, hundreds of regional traditional costumes, and everyday articles such as tools, decorative items, and jewellery made of wood, metal and ceramics. Most interesting are the re-creations of rooms complete with furniture, soft furnishings and utensils.

The museum also has displays on the ethnography of other cultures, with quality pieces brought back by the seafarers, scholars and explorers who

Zagreb

Botanički Vrt (the Botanical Gardens) offer an oasis of calm within the city

travelled to Old and New World lands in the Far East and South America, including tribal and religious masks, costumes and figures.

Mažuranićev trg 14. Tel: (01) 482 6220; www.etnografski-muzej.hr. Open: Tue–Thur 10am–6pm, Fri–Sun 10am–1pm. Admission fee.

Moderna galerije
(Gallery of Modern Art)

This gallery charts the changes in the Modernist movement in Croatia, concentrating on pieces that form the pivotal moment in an artist's development or in the development of a theory or school. The Friends of the Arts Society started the collection with just three works. It is now housed in the Vranyczany Mansion, home to the society's founder, Baron Vranyczany. The gallery has more than 10,000 items, including works by all the leading Croatian artists of the last 200 years.

Hebrangova 1. Tel: (01) 492 2368. Open: Tue–Sat 10am–6pm, Sun 10am–1pm. Admission fee.

Muzej Mimara (Mimara Museum)

Businessman Ante Topić Mimara was a prodigious collector of fine arts, antiques and antiquary objects. When he died in 1987 he donated his life's work to the city of Zagreb, and it is now housed in a vast neo-Renaissance building that was originally the city high school (1895).

This vast collection comprises over 3,750 items, with an important catalogue of Egyptian and Classical Greek pieces, priceless carpets from Persia and China, plus paintings and sculpture of which any national gallery would be proud. Artists represented include Canaletto, Constable, Raphael, Rembrandt, Renoir, Rodin, Rubens, Turner and Van Dyck.

Rooseveltov trg 4. Tel: (01) 482 8100. Open: Tue, Wed, Fri, Sat 10am–5pm, Thur 10am–7pm, Sun 10am–2pm. Admission fee.

Muzej za Umjetnost i Obrt (Arts and Crafts Museum)

The Arts and Crafts Museum is housed in a mansion designed by Bollé, a part of the great renaissance and expansion of Zagreb after the earthquake. It focuses not just on the applied arts of Croatia, but also those of much of continental Europe: it's like wandering through an interior design studio selling the best of everything fashioned by the finest craftsmen during the last 500 years, including cut glass from Bohemia, tapestries from Flanders and porcelain from Limoges.

Trg maršala Tita 10. Tel: (01) 482 2111; www.muo.hr. Open: Tue–Sat 10am–7pm, Sun 10am–2pm. Admission fee.

Strossmayerova Galerija Starih Majstora (The Strossmayer Gallery of Old Masters)

Displayed within the neo-Renaissance palace that is the seat of the Croatian Academy of Arts and Sciences, the Strossmayer Gallery comprises a number of important paintings by European artists, including works by

Strossmayer statue at the Gallery of Old Masters

El Greco, Goya, Dürer and Courbet. But its strength lies in its collection of Italian religious works which encompass the transition from Romanesque to Baroque artistic styles.

The gallery was set up using a donation by the Bishop Strossmayer of Đakovo in 1884, but has been enhanced by other private donations in the intervening years. Outside the building stands a sculpture of Strossmayer by Ivan Meštrović.

Trg N Zrinskog 11. Tel: (01) 489 5117; www.mdc.hr/strossmayer. Open: Tue 10am–1pm & 5–7pm, Wed–Sun 10am–1pm. Admission fee.

GREATER ZAGREB

The suburbs of modern Zagreb stretch into the distance to the south of the historic centre. To the north, Mount Medvednica has restrained most development, except for a few upmarket suburbs. Medvednica is Zagreb's playground, providing excellent walking in the summer. In the winter the Sljeme cable car whisks you to the upper elevations for skiing.

Groblje Mirogoj (Mirogoj Cemetery)

Cemeteries are not usually top of the tourist agenda, but Zagreb's Mirogoj, on the southern flank of Medvednica, is an exceptional place, where a great number of Croatia's political and cultural luminaries have found a final resting place. It is well worth a visit. The architect Hermann Bollé

(1845–1926) designed the cemetery in 1876, creating a neo-Renaissance-style garden laid out in a series of leafy squares. Two long, ivy-festooned arcades shelter the entrances to family tombs. The cemetery acts almost as a sculpture park, featuring works by the most renowned 20th-century Croatian sculptors, including Ivan Meštrović. *Mirogoj. Open: dawn–dusk.*

Trams trundle along grand avenues

SIGHTSEEING TOURS

There are daily guided tours of Zagreb, with varying itineraries, among them a bus tour of the greater city, and walking tours of Gornji Grad that include a visit to a traditional coffee house. Contact the tourist information office for full details.

THE ZAGREB CARD

The Zagreb Card allows free travel on public transport, including the funicular to the old city and the Sljeme cable car to Mt Medvednica. It also offers a 50 per cent discount on entrance fees for most of the major museums, the Zagreb sightseeing tours and certain car parks. Other benefits are a 10–20 per cent discount at participating theatres, shops, restaurants, car rental companies and nightclubs. Each card covers one adult and one child under 12 and is valid for either 24 or 72 hours from the time of sale. Cards are available from tourist information centres and some hotels at a cost of 60kn for a 24-hour card or 90kn for a 72-hour card; or buy them online at *www.zagrebcard-fivestars.hr* (currently only Visa and American Express are accepted).

Tourist information can be obtained at the following locations:
Trg bana J. Jelačića 11
Tel: (01) 481 4051

Trg N S Zrinskog 14
Tel: (01) 492 1645
www.zagreb-touristinfo.hr

PUBLIC TRANSPORT

Bus and tram tickets 8kn when bought from the driver, 6.5kn when pre-bought from newsstands. Day tickets 18kn. Funicular 3kn. Website for all trams and funicular *www.zet.hr* and for buses *www.akz.hr*

Neo-Renaissance gallery at Mirogoj Cemetery

Maksimirški Perivoj (Maksimir Park)

Zagreb's largest open space was laid out in 1794 in the style of Capability Brown, with lakes and woodland in addition to more formal elements. The park plays host to Zoološki vrt (the Zoo), which has a range of exotic species and native animals and birds.
Zoološki vrt. Tel: (01) 230 2199;
www.zoo.hr. Open: summer daily
9am–6pm (ticket office closes at 5pm);
winter daily 9am–4pm (ticket office
closes at 3pm). Admission fee.
Maksimirška Česta.
Open 24 hours.

Walk: A stroll from Gornji Grad to Donji Grad

To best appreciate Zagreb, it's important to sample the contrasts between Gornji Grad (Upper Town) and Donji Grad (Lower Town). This walk explores both, through the museums and attractions but also through the local 'atmosphere' that museums won't always supply.

Allow: 6 hours (including museum visits).

Start at the tourist information office on Trg bana Jelačić, the main square of the city. Turn right and walk out of the square along Bakačeva, where after 300m (1,000ft) you'll find the Cathedral of St Stephen on the right.

1 Cathedral of the Assumption

With its exceptional neo-Gothic façade, the cathedral is one of the finest churches in Croatia.

Cross the road, where a narrow alley leads to Dolac, the bustling main produce market for the city. Take Skalinska out at the far end of the market to Tkalčićeva, an atmospheric old street of bars and cafés. Take a right then left at Kravi Most to reach Radićeva. Turn right here and after 200m (660ft) you'll see the steps on the left at the bronze statue that take you to Kamenita Vrata (Stone Gate) and into Gornji Grad.

2 Kamenita vrata (Stone Gate)

Stone Gate is the last remaining gate into old Gradec. It incorporates a small

chapel where you always find votive candles burning and people in reflection and at prayer.

Once through the gate, walk straight across one junction to Markov Trg.

3 Markov Trg

The political heart of Croatia, Markov trg is home to the Croatian parliament building, but much more interesting for the visitor is St Mark's Church, with its highly colourful ceramic tiled roof and Gothic portal.

Leave the square via Čirilometodska and walk down 200m (660ft) to Lotrščak Tower on the right.

4 Lotrščak Tower

A 13th-century defensive tower, Lotrščak now offers one of the best vantage points in the city. The gun is fired every day at noon.

Just in front of the tower is the funicular railway. Take this quaint service down to Donji Grad. A short alleyway links the funicular to Ilica, the main shopping street of the city. Cross here and walk right. Take a left along Gundulićeva, then a right on Masarykova to reach Trg Maršala Tita. Cross the square to Rooseveltov Trg. The Mimara Museum is across the street.

The Art Pavilion on Tomislavov Trg

5 Mimara Museum

The high-quality collection, which was put together by industrialist Ante Mimara, rivals that of many national museums, and includes exquisite art and ancient artefacts.

Re-cross Rooseveltov Trg to the Ethnographic Museum.

6 Ethnographic Museum

Enjoy a comprehensive collection of traditional costumes, handicrafts and re-created lifestyles from Croatia, plus interesting ethnic items from various parts of the New World.

Take a right from the museum down Runjaninova until you meet the intersection of Vodnikova/Mihanovićeva.

The corner of the Botanical Gardens is across the street to the left.

7 Botanical Gardens

With over 10,000 plant species from around the world, these gardens are a must for gardening enthusiasts.

Turn down Mihanovićeva, past the Esplanade Hotel to Tomislavov Trg, the most beautiful of the squares, with its statue of King Bela and the neo-classical Art Pavilion.

Walk north through the square across Trankova to Strossmayerov Trg, where you'll find the Strossmayer Gallery of Old Masters.

8 Strossmayer Gallery of Old Masters

This comprises a collection of religious art chronicling the developments in the genre from the 14th to the 19th century.

From Strossmayerov Trg walk north across Zrinjevac Trg. Cross Teslina to leave the 'green horseshoe' of parks and make your way down Praška to complete the loop.

Walk: A stroll from Gornji Grad to Donji Grad

Istria

The northwestern corner of Croatia is a triangular-shaped piece of land pointing down the Adriatic from its head. A glorious land of vineyards and sentinel pines, it's reminiscent of Tuscany – but without the neat hedgerows and fresh paint that make its Italian cousin seem a little too manicured and primped. Offshore islands flank the rocky coastline and numerous coves, while man has played his part in the scattering of medieval fortified towns, Venetian harbours and modern resorts and marinas – playgrounds for today's tourists.

Istria was the heartland of ancient Illyrian territory. In the late 1st century it was ruled by many different feudal overlords before being absorbed into the Venetian empire – though much later than Dalmatia. Many noble families figure in the tangled web of Istrian history.

The influence of Italy is stronger in Istria than anywhere else in Croatia. The region was ruled by Italy between the two world wars, and did not become part of Yugoslavia until 1947. The spoken Croatian here has a definite Italian lilt. On street- and road-signs the names are given in Croatian with the Italian name in brackets.

Province-wide tourist information can be found on *www.istra.hr*

Bale (Valle)

Where tourists now swim and snorkel, dinosaurs once roamed. We know this because their bones have been unearthed just offshore by diving palaeontologists: huge brachiosauruses more than 20m (66ft) long. The Town Hall has a room with displays devoted to the Leviathan creatures found in the area.

In the 15th century the town was the fiefdom of the Soardo family, who built an immense fortified mansion that stayed in the family (through marriage to the Bembo name) until the 20th century. Currently undergoing a long programme of restoration, the mansion dominates a now sleepy village. Its vast façade – part fortress, part villa – has two fine mullioned Renaissance windows, while a gabled archway leads into the heart of the citadel.

11km (7 miles) southwest of Rovinj. Tourist information: Rovinjska 1. Tel: (052) 824 270; www.bale-valle.hr. Town Hall, Trg Bembo. Tel: (052) 824 303. Open: Mon–Fri 8am–1pm. Admission fee.

Barban

The Venetians sold the village of Barban to the Loredan family in 1535. It was already fortified, but they adapted it further to suit their needs, building a palace in the early 17th century with a fine loggia. The northern wall of the old citadel was incorporated into the Church of Sveti Nikola (St Nicholas) during the 18th century.

The village has recently reintroduced the medieval sport of *Trka na prstenac* (Tilting at the Ring), in which riders on horseback charge at rings hung from a pole. They must stick a ring with their lance in order to win the contest.
32km (20 miles) north of Pula. No tourist information.

Buje (Buie)

Set on a hilltop inland from the west coast, Buje is on the main road from Slovenia. It is often bypassed by tourists heading to Rovinj or Poreč, but it's certainly worth taking time out to explore the streets in the old town, once a medieval citadel. The narrow streets and alleyways lead inexorably to the old castle, but the highest point in the town is the top of the bell tower of Sv Servul (St Servol) Parish Church. Built on the

Traditional shuttered village houses at Bale

Church towers pierce the Istrian skies

site of a Roman temple in the 16th century (many stelae and columns were incorporated into the building), it was given a Baroque facelift in the 18th century, when the original three naves were incorporated into one grand nave, offering a vast space for its many altars. Strangely, the façade was never finished. *13km (8 miles) west of Umag. Tourist information: Istarska 2. Tel: (052) 773 353; www.tzg-buje.hr*

Fažana (Fasana)

Main jumping-off point for the Brijuni Islands National Park (*see p138*), the tiny port at Fažana bustles with small boats coming and going. Although it was settled in ancient times, little evidence of this remains. The simple Sveti Kuzma i Damjan (Saints Cosmas and Damian) Church overlooks the

fishing port. It contains a range of 16th-century frescoes and a well-regarded *Last Supper* dated 1578. *8km (5 miles) north of Pula. Tourist information: Riva 2. Tel: (052) 383 727.*

Grožnjan (Grisignana)

This tiny circular fortified hilltop village stands on a promontory high above a verdant valley. It is one of the best examples of medieval town planning in Istria. Sections of the original walls, including a 16th-century city gate, have been preserved to the present day. These now help protect a thriving artists' colony. The architectural highlights are the Baroque Sv Marij, Sv Vid and Sv Mod (St Mary's, St Vitus's and St Modest's) Church, which has some interesting carved choir stalls, and the Renaissance loggia.

The town plays host to a centre for musical youth and has performances throughout the summer. *14km (9 miles) east of Buje. Tourist information: Umberta Gorjana 3. Tel: (052) 776 131; www.groznjan-grisignana.hr/tz*

Labin

Ignore the rather ugly modern outskirts of Labin, which were built for a 20th-century mining community, and you'll be rewarded by the old town. Set on a rocky knoll, with far-reaching views around upper Istria, it has been fortified since Illyrian times and was an important outpost for the Romans and the Venetians.

The square at the base of the old town has several Venetian buildings, including a bastion and loggia. Set off on foot through the impressive 16th-century Sv Florus (St Flora) Gate – look out for the Lion of Venice on the inner gable – and amongst the concentric streets leading up to the pinnacle you'll find some impressive patrician palaces. Best of the Renaissance examples is the 15th-century Scampicchio, while the 18th-century Baroque palace of Battiala-Lazzarini is now home to the Labin Town Museum. This houses a gallery of artworks from the palace, as well as an ethnological collection and biographical information on Matthias Flacius Illyricus, native of the town and associate of Martin Luther. In the same square as the museum is the 14th-century Rodjenje Mariljino (Deliverance of the Virgin) Church, which contains a series of Venetian oils and Baroque styling from the 17th century.

42km (26 miles) north of Pula. Tourist information: Aldo Negro 20.
Tel: (052) 855 560. Labin Town Museum, Trg 1 Maja 6. Tel: (052) 852 477. Open: June–Sept daily 10am–1pm & 6–9pm; Oct–May Mon–Fri 10am–3pm. Admission fee.

Limski Canal

Just north of Rovinj, the Limski (also known as Lim Bay, Limski Bay or Lim Channel) is a karst limestone gorge 10km (6 miles) long and up to 500m (1,640ft) wide that opens out into the Adriatic. Here, the white rock reflects through the water, producing a whole spectrum of greens and blues. There are numerous grottoes to explore, and the larger Romuald's cave, where it is thought Romualdo, founder of the Benedictine monastery of St Michael, lived as a hermit. The ruins of the monastery can also be seen on the hillside on the northern bank.

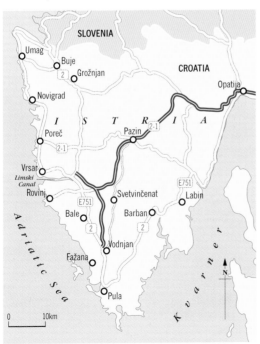

The whole 'canal' is now protected as a special marine reserve, and there is limited road access. It is best seen by boat, and numerous companies from resorts such as Rovinj and Vrsar offer trips including lunch and swimming.

Inland the gorge continues as a dry valley – the river flows through limestone caves underground – and here the evocative ruins of a medieval citadel, Dvigrad, abandoned to plague in the 17th century, watch over a lost river.

5km (3 miles) north of Rovinj. No tourist information.

Novigrad (Cittanova)

Although the name Novigrad means new town, this settlement dates from the 7th century, when the Byzantines expanded out of the confines of the Greek and Roman boundaries to create Neopolis.

The town was a bishopric from the end of the first millennium, and the site of a large monastery. This, and its economic strength as a port, brought it many treasures; sadly, these were lost in a devastating raid by the Turks in 1687. Novigrad lost its status as a see in 1831, so Sv Pelagij (St Peligo's or Pelagius's), also dedicated to St Mary and St Maximillian, which was once a cathedral, is now simply a church. Following a renovation to its original 13th-century form in the mid-1770s, it now boasts a combination of Gothic and Baroque elements. Some sections of the old town fortifications with their crenellated walls can still be found protecting the core of historic Novigrad. Within, amongst more humble family homes, are several palaces, including the

Novigrad's pretty harbour, lined with fishing boats

Baroque Riga mansion (1760).
15km (9¹/₂ miles) north of Poreč.
Tourist information: Porporella 6.
Tel: (052) 757 145.

Pazin

Site of Istria's most impressive
medieval fortress, and heartland of
anti-Venetian and anti-Turk
sentiments, Pazin was linked closely
with the Habsburgs. It was they who
funded the changes in the fortifications
above the 130m- (426ft-) high Fojba
Abyss from the 12th until the 18th
centuries in order to keep pace with the
developing weaponry of warfare,
though the basic layout has changed
little since 1540. The design of four
curtain walls around a central
courtyard oozes strength and power.
The main impression is of impregnable
walls of stone, though the few windows
offer a glimpse of the citadel's
evolution, displaying Romanesque,
Gothic and Renaissance styles. Today
the castle's more benign role is to host
the Etnografski muzej Istre I Zavičajni
Museji Pazinska (Istria Ethnological
Museum and Pazin Town Museum)
with a collection of traditional crafts,
costumes and handicrafts. Within the
old town, lying in the shadow of the
citadel, it's worth visiting the Sveti
Nikola (St Nicholas) Parish Church,
which has also developed over the
centuries. Originally erected in 1266,
the first upgrade came in 1441 with the
installation of a Gothic presbytery
decorated with magnificent frescoes.

It was embellished with Baroque
touches in 1764.
35km (22 miles) east of Poreč. Tourist
information: Franine I Jurine 14. Tel:
(052) 622 460; www.tzpazin.hr

Poreč (Parenzo)

Settled since the Neolithic period,
Poreč, which stands on a narrow
peninsula, was an important Roman
garrison. Later, during the first
millennium, it developed as an early
Christian community and an influential
bishopric. It chose Venetian rule over
that of Byzantium in 1267, the first
Istrian town to do so. The town's street
plan followed that of the Roman
castrum (fortified settlement) of
Colonia Julia Parentium, though the
streets now feature some exceptional
Romanesque, Gothic, Renaissance
and Baroque architecture, styles
that run the gamut of the centuries.
There are many on Decumanska (or
Decumanus), the main east–west
thoroughfare, though just about every
street or square has a gem or two. The
Zavičajni Museji Porečtine (Poreč Town
Museum) is housed in the 17th-century
Baroque Sinčić Palace, and has
interesting displays on the historical
development of the town. There's also a
small aquarium, with a variety of native
and tropical fish. Trg Marafor, at the
seaward end of the street, was the site
of the Roman forum.

Sv Eleuterija (Basilica of Euphrasius)
is the highlight of the town. A 6th-
century, early Christian religious

complex, it has some of the finest and most complete original mosaics of that era in the world. The site's importance was recognised by UNESCO, and it has been protected since 1997 as a World Heritage Site. The remains of four churches can be found here. The last is the 6th-century basilica dedicated to Euphrasius, who was bishop of Poreč at that time. The church is an exceptional example of the early Byzantine three-apse and three-nave plan, supported by two rows of slender marble columns, whose original ornate capitals and polychrome stucco reliefs can still be seen on the left-hand side as you stand in the church doorway.

The *pièce de résistance* is the central apse at the far end of the church. Gold leaf and mosaics fill the entire wall space. In the cupola, Mother and Child are flanked by Croatian Christian martyrs, including Euphrasius himself. This is the oldest extant depiction of the Virgin Mary in the world. Medallions depicting the saints can be seen on the underside of the arch, while in a border above the apse, Christ is flanked by the Apostles. The window level of the apse depicts scenes from the Bible, including the Annunciation and the Visitation. All the mosaics have an extremely lifelike quality that would have been revolutionary for their time. The flow and movement in the scenes mark a high point in eastern mosaic composition. Just inside the door on the left and right are sections of mosaics from the earlier church on the site.

The on-site museum allows you to view larger mosaics from the 4th-century Mauro's Oratory. This was built by Bishop Mauros, patron saint of Poreč, who was martyred by Emperor Diocletian (*see pp92–3*). There is also a collection of oil-on-wood triptychs. You can climb the 16th-century bell tower for fine views over the town. *60km (37½ miles) northwest of Pula. Tourist information: Zagrebačka 9. Tel: (052) 451 293. Aquarium, F. Glavinića 4. Tel: (052) 482 720; www.aquarium-porec.com. Open: daily Apr–Oct 9am–9pm, Nov–Mar 10am–5pm. Admission fee. Poreč Town Museum, Decumanska 9. Tel: (052) 431 585. Open: June–Sept 10am–1pm & 6–9pm. Closed Oct–May. Admission fee. Sv Eleuterija (Basilica of Euphrasius). Open: daily 10am–7pm. Free. Museum and bell tower. Open: daily 10am–7pm. Admission fee.*

Pula (Pola)

Economic 'capital' of Istria, and its largest city, Pula was an important naval port into the 20th century. Its large docks now play host to commercial sea traffic. It is too much of a hotchpotch of architectural styles to be described as handsome, but its collection of Roman edifices and compact old town, plus its bustling atmosphere, make it a must for a day or half-day trip – which most tourists make from other resorts around the region.

Pula was one of the most important settlements in the Roman Balkans

The magnificent frescoes of Sv Eleuterija (Basilica of Euphrasius) at Poreč

region, as witnessed by what is still the highlight of the town, the Roman Amphitheatre. One of the largest in Europe, this 23,000-seater auditorium was completed in *c* AD 79 and used for gladiatorial contests and cultural events. The theatre seems to have survived almost intact until the interior stone was recycled, principally for the castle (*see below*). What remains today is essentially the shell of the building, the outer wall, with three floors on the seaward side topped with an upper walkway. The archways around the wall allowed light to penetrate internal walkways, from where spectators would enter the arena to find their seats.

An interesting museum in the underground vaults contains original artefacts such as amphorae and inscribed tablets. The theatre is still used for concerts throughout the summer, though with all the original seating gone, the capacity has dropped to a mere 5,000.

The social centre of Pula is still the Forum, also built by the Romans. Here there is another smaller – though no less impressive – Roman remain, the 1st century AD Augustov hram (Temple of Romae and Augustus), elegant in its simplicity, with an archetypal portico topped with an ornate pediment. Beside the temple is the Gothic Town Hall, completed in 1296 and still in use today. Two gates of the Roman city still stand. Herculova vrata (Gate of Hercules) is the older – 1st century BC – with a neat, unadorned façade, while

the 2nd-century AD Dvojna vrata (Twin Gate) is much more flamboyant. By far the most ornate arch is Slavoluk obitelji Sergijevaca (Arch of Sergii), not a city gate but a triumphal arch erected in the 1st century BC to commemorate the achievements of a local family.

Not surprisingly, Roman artefacts dominate the Arheološki muzej Istre (Istrian Archaeology Museum). The vast collection comprises all the trappings of daily life, from cooking utensils to fine jewellery, plus some monumental statuary. It's well worth a visit to gain an insight into the real sophistication of Roman society.

The descriptions of Pula's churches read like a history of church architecture. The oldest is the tiny, 6th-century Kapela Sv Marije Formoze (St Mary of Formosa), once an inner chapel of a larger early Romanesque basilica, while Sveti Frane (St Francis) Church displays a Gothic form. Though much of the Katedrala (Cathedral of the Ascension of the Virgin) dates from the 17th century, the simple nave indicates its earlier, first millennium AD origins.

Atop the highest point in Pula, there's been a fortress for centuries. The main elements of the citadel you see today – four triangular bastions with a central core – date from the 14th century, when the Byzantines kept their western fleet in the harbour below. It was developed in the 1630s to a design by French naval architect Antoine de Ville. The fortress is home to the

Provijesni muzej Istre (Provincial Museum).
35km (22 miles) south of Rovinj.
Arheološki muzej Istre, Carrarina 3.
Tel: (052) 218 603. Open: May–Sept daily 9am–8pm; Oct–Apr Mon–Fri 9am–3pm. Admission fee.
Provijesni muzej Istre. Tel: (052) 211 740. Open: May–early Sept daily 8am–9pm; mid-Sept–end Apr Mon–Fri 9am–5pm, Sat & Sun 10am–1pm. Admission fee.
Roman Amphitheatre, Flavijevska. Tel: (052) 219 028. Open: daily

Taking a stroll in the Roman Amphitheatre, Pula

10am–7pm. Admission fee.
Audio guide.
Tourist information: Forum 3.
Tel: (052) 212 987; www.pulainfo.hr

Rovinj (Rovigno)

Rovinj is one of Croatia's most magical places. A dewdrop-shaped isthmus contains a fascinating old town that just oozes character, while the 18th-century 'new' town presents the perfect panorama of pastel façades.

The old town was originally an island lying only metres offshore. It was fortified in the 7th century and developed into a tangle of narrow streets carpeted with marble blocks worn smooth through the ages. There's real life to be found here around the narrow, five-storey apartment houses, some dating back to the 16th century: kids play football; women coo over babies; washing hangs like bunting from every tiny window. The buildings are a pleasing mix of family homes, café bars and artists' galleries. The galleries offer a great chance to buy souvenirs – or simply engage in some serious browsing.

Overlooking the old town is Sveta Eufemija (St Euphemia) Church, built in style in the mid-18th century, though the Venetian Baroque façade was added a century later. The 60m (197ft) tower offers splendid views down over the terracotta-tiled rooftops of the old town and out into the bay beyond, but the wooden stairs are not for the faint-hearted. For those with a fear of heights, the terrace around the church gives some idea of what you're missing.

In the 18th century the town spilled out across the narrow channel to the mainland; land was reclaimed and Rovinj became permanently linked to Istria. Many sections of the old town walls were demolished and the narrow Baroque stone Balbjev luk (Balbi's Gate) now marked the entrance to the old town. The new town, with its wider streets and numerous miniature piazzas, is crammed with shops and cafés. The Town Hall, with its characteristic loggia, plays host to the Rovinj Heritage Museum, housing an eclectic collection of artefacts (Roman to medieval) and art (15th- to 19th-

ST EUPHEMIA

In AD 800 a late Roman stone sarcophagus 'floated' into the harbour at Rovinj. When it was opened, the townsfolk found the body of Euphemia in a perfect state of preservation, despite the fact that she had died as a Christian martyr more than 500 years before. She was proclaimed patron saint of the town and her remains lie in St Euphemia Church.

century paintings and sculpture). You'll also find a small aquarium at Obala Giordano Paliaga 5.

For the evening *passeggiata*, Rovinj has a harbour that puts St Tropez to shame. Terracotta and mustard façades glow in the rays of the setting sun; instead of members of the jet set, you'll find an unpretentious crowd from all

The pastel façades and palm trees of Rovinj harbour

Fishing plays an important role in the Croatian economy

across Europe, strolling and admiring the yachts or pausing for an aperitif at one of the many cafés. Five hundred metres (1,640ft) offshore in the bay of Rovinj is the island of Sveta Katarina (St Katherine's), another popular destination for a stroll, especially in the oppressive heat of summer. The island is a botanist's delight, with more than 450 plant species. (*See also Zlatni Rt, p146.*) *35km (22 miles) northwest of Pula. Aquarium, Obala Giordano Paliaga 5. Tel: (052) 804 712. Open: Apr–June & Sept–Oct 10am–5pm; July–Aug 9am–9pm. Admission fee. Ferries to St Katherine's run every hour from 6am–11pm (peak season only: ferries will be fewer mid-Sept–mid-May and may not run in bad weather).*

Sveta Eufemija (St Euphemia) Tower. Garibaldijeva 1. Tel: (052) 815 615. Open: daily 8am–7pm. Admission fee. Tourist information: Pino Budicin 12. Tel: (052) 811 566; www.tzrovinj.hr. Rovinj Heritage Museum; Trg M Tita 11. Tel: (052) 816 720; www.muzej-rovinj.com. Open: mid-June–mid-Sept Tue–Sun 9am–noon & 7–10pm; mid-Sept–mid-June, Tue–Sat 9am–1pm. Admission fee.

Svetvinčenat

This tiny central Istrian village is dominated by a monumental Venetian citadel (currently being renovated). Erected by the Grimani family in the medieval era, the Morisini family added a Renaissance wing to the structure in

The slow pace of life at Svetvinčenat

the 15th century. The result is impressive yet rather odd, as if two halves of different castles have been fused together. In the square outside the castle entrance are several Renaissance buildings, including an elegant loggia and the Church of the Annunciation.

20km (12¹/₂ miles) east of Rovinj.
Tourist information:
Svetvinčenat 47.
Tel: (052) 560 005.

Umag (Umago)

Least pleasing of western Istria's coastal resorts, Umag nonetheless has the region's ubiquitous old town – albeit a small one – with narrow alleyways and 17th-century stone buildings. Set on a narrow isthmus, it's a little more careworn than neighbouring Poreč and Rovinj, but for those who prefer their architecture 'lived in', there are lots of special little historical features, including some incredible Renaissance windows and doorways.

In the Middle Ages Umag belonged to Trieste (now in northern Italy) but it later fell under Venetian control. Just outside the medieval quarter is Sveta Marija (St Mary of the Ascension) Church, a good example of Venetian Baroque (begun in 1730), with a large selection of canvases in the many side chapels. The tower-like belfry, built in 1691, watches over the rather nondescript main square, Trg Slobode.

15km (9¹/₂ miles) north of Novigrad. Tourist information: Trgovačka 6. Tel: (052) 741 363.

Vodnjan (Dignano)

Vodnjan is the setting for the tallest church in Istria, the 18th-century Svetog Blaža (Church of St Blaise), modelled on the Church of San Pietro in Castello in Venice. A monumental construction for such a small parish, the detached belfry is more than 60m (197ft) high.

The church houses a great collection of religious relics, liturgical instruments and treasures, and paintings that include the polyptych of Bishop Leon Bembo by Paolo Veneziano (dating from 1321), and a later Renaissance triptych by Lazar Bastiani. Most interesting, though a little bizarre, are the bodies of important clergy, displayed in glass cases, which are known as the 'Vodnjan mummies'. Among these is the body of St Nikola of Kopar.

12km (7¹/₂ miles) north of Pula. Tourist information: Trg Narodni 3. Tel: (052) 511 700. Svetog Blaža, Trg Sveti Blaz. Tel: (052) 511 420. Open: daily 9am–7pm. Admission fee.

Vrsar (Orsera)

Set on a small coastal knoll just north of the mouth of the Limski Canal, Vrsar overlooks several bays that have been settled since Illyrian times. In the 5th century a Christian religious complex was founded here, but only the floor mosaics have survived to the present day. Later the town came under the jurisdiction of the Bishops of Poreč.

The Romanesque St Mary of the Sea Church crowns the town. Today the marina plays host to some of the finest maritime craft in the Adriatic, bobbing happily alongside the tiny wooden fishing boats that service the restaurants along the waterfront.

12km (7¹/₂ miles) south of Poreč. Tourist information: Rade Končara 46. Tel: (052) 441 187.

Zlatni Rt Park Forest (see p146)

Walk: Discovering Roman Pula

It is an adventure in time-travel as you stroll Pula's streets. Roman, Gothic, Renaissance and Baroque architecture sit happily side by side, surrounded by the trappings of 21st-century life – you'll never be short of somewhere to relax and have a drink or a snack. The Roman thread will serve to lead you through the city, but don't neglect its other historical charms.

Allow: 3 hours with visits. Start at the Slavoluk obitelji Sergijevaca (Arch of Sergii).

1 Slavoluk obitelji Sergijevaca (Arch of Sergii)

Although this was never a city gate (it was a triumphal arch erected to commemorate rather than allow access), it forms a present-day boundary between 'modern' Pula and the Venetian old town. As befits a celebratory edifice, it is ornately decorated and inscribed.

From the arch walk down ul Sergijevaca,

The Roman Slavoluk obitelji Sergijevaca (Arch of Sergii) marks the boundary of old Pula

now a main shopping street but with fine 16th- and 17th-century façades. Follow the road until you reach the Forum.

2 The Forum

The site of the Roman Forum has retained its name to this day; it is still an open space, now filled with cafés. Directly ahead on the opposite side of the square is the Gothic Town Hall, and beside that stands the Temple of Romae and Augustus, built at the heart of the Roman city in the 1st century AD.

Retrace your steps and take one of the cobbled lanes that cut left off Sergijevaca – either Ul Sv Pranje or Ul Vicenta iz Kastiva – to reach Ul Castropola, which follows a circular route. Turn left and walk until you reach a right turn (Gradinski Upson), which heads up to the summit. Take this street. A narrow, steep flight of steps will lead you to the summit, which is dominated by the Venetian Castro (castle).

3 The Castro

On the far side of the Castro are the scant remains of a small 2nd-century AD Roman amphitheatre.

Return to Ulica Castropolo and bear left to the far side of the summit. Here you'll find the Archaeological Museum.

4 Arheološki muzej (Archaeological Museum)

The museum holds important collections of artefacts – masses of everyday items that that reveal the richness of life in Roman Pula. The collection really puts meat on the bones of the extant monumental remains such as the temples and the amphitheatre.

Leave the museum by bearing left out of the front gardens.

5 Dvojna vrata (Twin Gate)

You'll depart under the Twin Gate with its two arches. This was erected in the late 2nd century AD at the eastern entrance to the city, but the roads it serviced have been lost to redevelopment.

Once under the arch, turn left on the street that runs parallel to it, Ulica Carrarina, until you reach the crossroads around 50m (160ft) away. Take a right on Amfiteatarska Ulica and you'll see the impressive curtain walls of the amphitheatre directly ahead.

Enjoying the view from the Castro walls

6 The Roman amphitheatre

The walls are almost intact – a splendid elliptical shape rising to a height of 30m (98ft) on the seaward side. None of the auditorium seating remains, but the interior dimensions give an impression of the size and complexity of the structure. Head to the underground rooms to explore the collections of amphorae and other finds.

Drive: From coast to coast across Istria

This full-day tour leads you on an adventure across the Istrian mainland, starting at a leading tourist resort on the Adriatic west coast and finishing on its east coast at the Bay of Rijeka. The trip takes you through some wonderful countryside, planted with vineyards, oak forests and scrubland thick with the heady aroma of wild herbs. There is also a host of pretty inland villages to explore, each with its own fascinating history. One word of caution: there are no road numbers to follow along the route, but the village names are well signposted.

Distance: 150km (93 miles). Allow: 8 hours.

Start your journey at Umag. Follow signs for 12km (7½ miles) to Buje.

1 Buje

This once-fortified town has a maze of streets to explore, with the church of St Servulus being an interesting amalgam of styles. Roman stelae are incorporated into its 16th–18th-century fabric.
Take the road from Buje to Triban. Once through Triban look out for the right turn signposted Grožnjan.

One of the fortified villages that are typical of the Istrian mainland

2 Grožnjan

This tiny enclave has now been transformed into an artists' colony, and its many galleries may tempt you to part with some cash early in the tour.
Retrace your steps to the intersection of the road to Triban, but now continue straight ahead to Marušici. At this village take a right and travel to Sterna, then follow signs to Sv Lucija. 1 km (just over ½ mile) up the hill beyond Sv Lucija, you'll arrive in Oprtalj.

3 Oprtalj

Set high on a hill and with panoramic views, Oprtalj is mainly visited for its churches. Head to the main square of the town, where you'll find St George's Church, a late Gothic building (1520s). Another great treasure is the Sveta Marija (St Mary's), a simple 15th-century chapel with frescoed panels on each wall of the nave, depicting scenes from the Bible.

Continue on from Oprtalj down the hill through Pirelici and over the Mirna River, where you'll reach a crossroads 7km (4½ miles) after leaving Oprtalj. Go straight across here to Motovun (Montona).

4 Motovun (Montona)

In the Middle Ages the settlement was at a crossroads of Istrian communications and trade, but it is a sleepy backwater today. The citadel walls (13th–15th century) remain intact around a tiny inner enclave topped by a simple Gothic bell tower.

Retrace your steps back to the crossroads and turn right following signs to Buzet.

5 Buzet

Centre of the Istrian truffle industry, the people of Buzet mostly live in the new town in the valley nowadays. Buzet still has a walled old town on the hilltop – it was on the border of Venetian territory – that is worth exploring.

Depart Buzet in the direction of Roč (also signposted Čiritez and Rijeka). Reach Roč after 8km (5 miles).

6 Roč

The remains of strong 14th-century walls are most evident at Roč. This part of Istria was the birthplace of Glagolitic writing, which eventually developed into the Cyrillic alphabet. In the narrow lane leading from Roč to the nearby village of Hum is now a modern 'sculpture trail', with early Glagolitic documents carved into stone stelae.

From Roč head to Rijeka. At the junction just past Lupoglava, after approximately 9km (5½ miles), turn right on the main road to Pazin.

7 Pazin

Explore the huge Pazin citadel, a main border-post between the Venetians and the Habsburgs.

From Pazin head east, following signs for Podpićan via Pićan, then south to Labin via Sv Nedelja and Vinez, before you reach your final destination, Rabac.

8 Rabac

Rabac takes advantage of the natural inlet on which it stands and has an excellent marina. It's the perfect place to enjoy a lazy meal after your day's activities.

Kvarner

Set around the head of Rijecki zajev (Rijeka Bay), and forming the coastal link between Istria and Dalmatia, Kvarner is probably the least-known Croatian region. The catchphrase of the Kvarner tourist authorities – 'Shores, Islands, Highland' – is a most appropriate one, however, and gives some indication of the sheer variety of the natural attractions on offer there.

A clutch of islands lies in the bay between Istria and the Kvarner mainland. Sparsely populated, they are dotted with fortified medieval settlements. Vast tracts of island land were the sole preserve of sheep until well into the 20th century. The *gromače,* or dry-stone walls, built by the shepherds to manage their flocks, are an overriding feature of the landscape.

While Venice held sway over the islands, the mainland was fought over by Hungary and the Ottoman Empire, and here a different Empire style of architecture is prevalent.

The hinterland boasts some exceptional highland and mountain scenery, exemplified in two of its best-known national parks, Plitvice Lakes and Risnjak (*see p143*). Tourism in Croatia began here, on the westernmost section of the Kvarner coast, when the Austro-Hungarian social elite began visiting to enjoy the fresh sea air in the late 19th century.

Bakar

What a shame that this fortified old town is now surrounded by rather ugly oil refineries, because the remains of the 16th-century Frankopan castle that crown the settlement are certainly worth exploring. The town has a long history. The Romans built a spa around the freshwater springs found at the head of this sheltered bay.

10km (6 miles) south of Rijeka. Tourist information: Primorje 39.
Tel: (051) 761 411.

Cres

The north of Cres (also known as Cherso) island is a barren landscape, heady with the scent of wild herbs, while the south is lusher. Until recently the island made a living from sheep farming. Nature-lovers may want to visit Beli, in the far north. This picturesque but remote village is headquarters of the Caput-Insulae Ecocentre, whose prime mission is to protect the colony of griffon vultures that inhabit the sea cliffs in the north. The main draw is to see the huge birds in the recuperation centre, but there's also information about the ecosystem of northern Cres.

Tiny Osor, the town closest to Lošinj (*see p69*), was the capital of the island until the 15th century, and was also an important early bishopric. Here you'll find a handful of Gothic and Renaissance buildings, including the old Cathedral of the Assumption and the Bishop's Palace with its rich frescoes. The Town Hall houses a small Arheološki musej (Archaeological Museum). Cres Town, the current 'capital', sits on a narrow bay, one third of the way down the island. One of the places least affected by tourism, it is nevertheless a pretty town of fishermen's cottages set around a sheltered harbour.

In the Bay of Rijeka. Arheološki Musej, Palazzo Petrić. Tel: (051) 571 127. Open: Apr–Sept daily 8am–7pm. Admission fee. Caput-Insulae Ecocentre, Beli. Tel: (051) 840 525. Open: May–Sept 9am–8pm, Oct–Apr 9am–5pm. Admission fee. Ferry connections with Lošinj at Mali Lošinj, the Istrian coast at Brestova, and Valbiska on Krk. Tourist information: Cons 10, Cres Town. Tel: (051) 571 535; www.tzg-cres.hr

Crikvenica

A major tourist resort on the Kvarner mainland, Crikvenica was the site of an important Pauline monastery housed in a castle built by Nikola Frankopan in the early 15th century. The complex was expanded several times before the dissolution of the order in the early 19th century, and the castle lay empty until it was converted into one of the

The inviting sea at the long bay in Baska on Krk island

The tiny medieval heart of Lovran

first tourist hotels along this part of the coast.

15km (9¹/2 miles) south of Rijeka. Tourist information: Trg S. Radića 1. Tel: (051) 241 051; www.tzg-crikvenice.hr

Krk

The largest of Croatia's offshore islands, Krk (also known as Veglia) was ruled by several powers throughout the first millennium before becoming the fiefdom of the Frankopan family. It was ruled directly from Venice from 1480–1797. The island is connected by a road-bridge to the mainland, but it also boasts an airport. There are regular summer charter flights to and from various European destinations.

The Romans settled the capital, Krk Town, but the Venetian city wall and city gates – set beside a small harbour – are the most obvious vestiges of its later history. Within the walls, the Cathedral of the Assumption has 11th-century elements, but has received several facelifts. Recent excavations around the cathedral have shown that it rests on the remains of the Roman baths, proving that Christianity was founded here in the earliest era. The adjacent museum contains other works from the cathedral and churches across the island. Just south of the capital, set on the small island of Košljun in the middle of an inlet, is a 15th-century Franciscan monastery, an important repository of Glagolitic texts. It's possible to tour the cloisters, the church and the treasury.

The fortified village of Omišalj lies close to the mainland. Among the narrow streets is the 13th-century Sv Marij (St Mary's) Church, with a 15th-century triptych. In the church square is a Venetian loggia.

In the far south of the island, the modern resort of Baška nestles around a long sandy bay. Just inland are the villages of Starigrad with the ruins of the 10th-century citadel, and Jurandvor, which holds a copy of the Baška Tablet, the oldest Glagolitic text ever discovered in Croatia.

25km (15¹/₂ miles) southwest of Rijeka by road. Tourist information: For the island at Trg Sv Kvirina 1, Krk Town. Tel: (051) 221 359; www.krk.hr. Local offices also at Baška.

Lošinj

Separated from Cres by the Kavuada Canal, the island of Lošinj (also known as Lussino) is a popular destination for holidaymakers. The island's main claims to fame are the magnificent beach at Čikat Bay, with its strands of protected ancient pine forest, and the busy main town, Mali Lošinj, which is near the beach.

Mali Lošinj is one of Croatia's major tourist resorts and the largest town on the island. It bears the hallmarks of Venetian rule but also thrived in the 19th century. The bustling seafront with its pastel façades is a popular place for the evening stroll, or *passeggiata*, before dinner.

By contrast, Veli Lošinj to the south is a much lower-key settlement, set around a slender coastal inlet.

In the Bay of Rijeka 3km (2 miles) south of Cres. Passenger ferry connections from Cres, Krk and Kraljevica, south of Rijeka. Tourist information: Riva lošinjskih kapetana 29, Mali Lošinj. Tel: (051) 231 547; www.tz-malilosinj.hr

Map of the Kvarner region showing SLOVENIA, E63, E65, A12, Opatija, Rijeka, Bakar, KVARNER, Lovran, Crikvenica, ISTRIA, E751, KRK, Krk, Baška, Cres, CRES, RAB, Rab, DALMATIA, Osor, LOSINJ, Mali Lošinj, Kvarner, Kvarneric

N

0   15km   - - - borders of Kvarner

Lovran

Lovran is the oldest town on the so-called 'Opatija Riviera' (*see opposite*). It was an important maritime port during the 12th century, later becoming part of the Pazin feudal domain. Some of the original medieval town walls remain, but bigger draws are the 16th- and 17th-century patrician houses that line the narrow alleyways. Sveti Juria (St George's) Church dates from the 12th century but was later extended. *35km (22 miles) west of Rijeka. Tourist information: Šetalište M Tita 63. Tel: (051) 291 740; www.tz-lovran.hr*

Opatija

This gracious town attracted the upper echelons of the Empire, who were keen to follow the new fashion for holidaying. Regular visits by Austrian royals cemented Opatija's reputation with the Habsburg '*beau monde*'.

Today the atmosphere in Opatija remains genteel, with lavish villas, manicured parks, seafront promenades and a range of high-class shopping. *25km (15¹/₂ miles) north of Rijeka. Tourist information: M. Tita 101/4. Tel: (051) 271 310; www.opatija-tourism.hr*

The gardens of the Villa Angiolina at Opatija

Rab

The smallest of Kvarner's main islands, Rab is popular with tourists, who are attracted by the lush vegetation and fine beaches. There's only one main town on the island, Rab, set on a narrow isthmus and recognisable for the four church bell towers that pierce the skyline. It is replete with architectural jewels, from Romanesque to Baroque – Rab has one of the densest concentrations of fine buildings in Croatia.

Sv Andrija (St Andrew's) Church is part of a Benedictine monastery begun in the early 12th century. Other religious buildings of importance are the island's major church, Katedral of Sv Marija Velika (Cathedral of St Mary the Great), consecrated 50 years after St Andrew's and an elegant design of pink and white stone. Sv Frane (St Francis's) Church dates from the 1490s, straddling Gothic and Renaissance styles, and Sv Antun (St Anthony's) Church displays pure Baroque design.

Knežev Dvor (Prince's Palace), begun in the 13th century but expanded during Venetian rule, is one of the best examples of secular architecture, though it is not open to the public. The palaces of the Cassio or Kukulić families are also impressive.

In the north of the island, at the head of a long narrow bay, Kampor has an excellent setting and a Franciscan monastery. Lopar, set on some fine beaches, is a growing tourist resort. *South of Krk. Ferry services from Rijeka,*

A neo-classical confection at Rijeka

*Baška on Krk and Jablanac on the Dalmatian mainland at Rab's southernmost point, Mišnjak.
Tourist information: Trg Municipium Arba 8, Rab Town. Tel: (051) 724 064; www.tzg-rab.hr. Also an office in Lopar.*

Rijeka

Given all the wonderful old port towns and island communities to explore, it's difficult to sell Rijeka as a tourist destination, but the central core has some excellent 18th- and 19th-century buildings, and there's a medieval hilltop citadel worthy of exploration.
*188km (117¹/₂ miles) west of Zagreb.
Tourist information: Korzo 33. Tel: (051) 335 882; www.tz-rijeka.hr*

Drive: Krk Island

The largest of Croatia's Adriatic islands at just over 400sq km (154sq miles), Krk offers a full and varied range of activities, including some established holiday resorts, characterful old towns, one of the most important religious reliquaries in Croatia, and a fortified capital with impressive stone walls.

Distance: 110km (69 miles) round trip.

Allow: 8 hours.

Cross the road bridge (toll) from the mainland near Kraljevica to start your trip. You'll pass the turn-off for the airport on your left before you see a sign on the right for Omišalj after 4km (2½ miles). Take this road into the village.

1 Omišalj

Set above its cosy fishing harbour, Omišalj is quite a large village that still has vestiges of its old medieval fortifications. Visit the 13th-century Sv Marija (St Mary's) Church at its heart.

Return to route 29 and continue south in the direction of Krk Town. After 8km (5 miles) take the right turn for Malinska.

2 Malinska

This well-developed tourist resort sits surrounded by verdant forest.

From Malinska return to route 29 and follow signs to Krk Town. You'll need to park your car on the harbour front before strolling into the old town.

3 Krk Town

The town walls are remarkably intact, heading back inland many hundreds of metres. You'll still need to enter through one of the three Venetian gates. The alleyways in the lower section of Krk are even more narrow and winding than usual in old Croatian towns, which can give it a slightly oppressive feeling. The harbour front has several cafés where you can take a break before continuing your journey.

Tour boats moored at Krk Town

From Krk Town head east on route 29 in the direction of Punat (it is also signposted for Baška). Be careful, because there are a couple of tight bends just as you come out of town. A coastal inlet appears on the right and you'll get your first glimpse of Košljun Island and its monastery. After 4km (2½ miles) turn right at the sign for Punat.

4 Košljun Island

Shuttle taxis depart from Punat to Košljun throughout the day – you'll see them on the quayside. Take the five-minute ride out to the island to explore the religious complex with its 15th-century buildings and collection of liturgical treasures, and stroll around the beautiful forest on the rest of the island.

Once back on Krk Island, retrace your route from Punat to the main island road (29), turn right and continue southeast along the backbone of the island. After 16km (10 miles) you'll reach the tiny village of Jurandvor.

5 Jurandvor

Stop at the parish church in Jurandvor to gaze on a copy of the earliest Glagolitic script written in Croatia. The original was found here but is now in Zagreb. The Glagolitic script later developed into the Cyrillic alphabet that is used throughout the Balkans today.

From Jurandvor carry on into Baška.

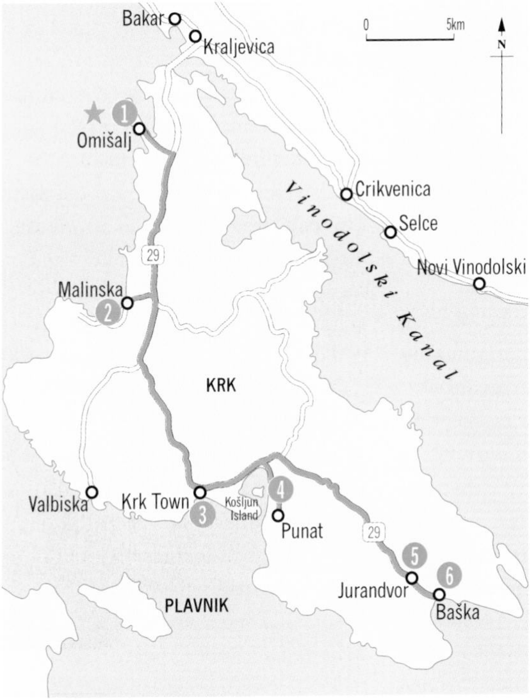

6 Baška

One of Kvarner's most popular holiday resorts, the old town of Baška nestles next to the shore on the northern side of the bay, sheltered from the prevailing bora wind. The modern resort stretches south, paralleling the long golden beach. This is the perfect place to enjoy some sunshine before you embark on your return journey.

Split and northern Dalmatia

In the heart of the Croatian Adriatic, Split and northern Dalmatia bring together culture and nature in an almost perfect combination. The very north of the region, beyond Zadar, is the least developed part of Croatia. It is a dramatically beautiful, almost barren landscape of limestone peaks, seen at their best in the Paklenica National Park (see pp141–2); the park protects an area of land comprising a ridge of dramatic white (limestone) peaks. A string of tiny settlements clings to the coastal strip.

In the more populated south, traditional vine production still continues. Vines are grown within sturdy stone enclaves to protect the plants and fruit from the bora wind and the desiccating summer sun.

The region has more than 300 islands, islets and reefs, offering sailors a perfect environment to unfurl the sail and catch the wind. The Kornati Islands National Park (*see pp139–40*) is an uninhabited paradise just waiting to be explored. Landlubbers are no less catered for, with some fine old Venetian ports to explore, countless breathtaking churches, plus the ancient remains of Salona and Split with their archaeological treasures.

Brač

Brač was the source of much of the stone that built the Venetian cities; it is still quarried today. The island was used as a summer retreat by the upper echelons of society from Roman Salona and Split. It later came under Venetian rule, but its building are relatively low-key compared with other island settlements. The old Governor's Palace stands at Nerežišća, the old capital in the centre.

Today the island is famed for one of the most dramatic and beautiful beaches in Europe, Zlatni rat, or Golden Horn, at Bol on the south coast. This pale strand sits like an arrowhead protruding from a forested headland; the tip is constantly changing due to winds, tides and currents. If you can drag yourself away from the beach, visit the Dominican monastery close to Bol village, which has a painting attributed to Tintoretto.

The highest point on the island, Vidova Gora, at 778m (1,552ft), is the perfect place for hiking, offering vast tracts of verdant pine forests.

25km (15½ miles) south of Split. Tourist information: Porat 1, Supetar. Tel: (021) 630 551; www.supetar.hr

Porat Bilskih Pomoraca, Bol. Tel: (021) 635 638; www.bol.hr
Ferry services from Split to Supetar and Makarska to Sumartin.

Hvar

One of the most popular holiday islands in the Adriatic, Hvar is long and slim, and lies almost perpendicular to the Dalmatian coast.

Hvar Town, the capital, sits on the southwest corner of the island. Ruled by Venice for many centuries, it was one of the first safe ports of call for ships travelling back home from the Orient. Today, its 13th-century crenellated town walls still guard many fine buildings. Rather like St Mark's in Venice, the town square opens onto the waterfront. It is home to the Renaissance Katedrala Sv Stjepena (Cathedral of St Stephen), with its elegant 17th-century bell tower. Also on the square, the clock tower, loggia and the Palača Hektorović (Hektorović Palace) all date from the 15th century, while the theatre was the first to be opened in Europe in 1612. Outside the city walls is the Franjevački Samostan (Franciscan Monastery), where the adjoining Gospa od Milosti (Our Lady of Charity) has a collection of Renaissance paintings.

Stari Grad in the north of the island was founded as early as the 4th century BC, but the major edifice is Kaštel Tvrdalj in the town's centre, the fortified home of poet Petar Hektorović (1487–1572), built c1520.

Tiny Vrboska boasts a fortified church, Sv Marija (St Mary's), which was designed to protect the residents in

Zlatni Rat on Brač is one of the finest beaches in Croatia

case of Ottoman attack. In the far east of the island, the remains of a ruined Venetian castle now gaze down on the village of Sućuraj and the ferry port.

Hvar is famed for its lavender, best seen during late May and June, when the air is heady with scent. You can buy many lavender products here, from soap to honey, and also a unique lace made from agave leaves.

40km (25 miles) south of Split. Ferry services Split to Hvar Town and Stari Grad, Drvenik (on the Dalmatian mainland) to Sućuraj. Also linked with Korčula island to the south, and to Vis and Dubrovnik.
Tourist information: Trg sv Stjepana, Hvar Town Tel: (021) 741 059, Nova Riva 2, Stari Grad. Tel: (021) 765 763.

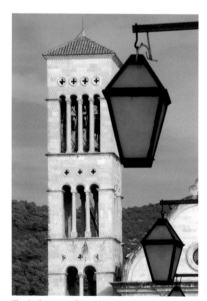

The bell tower of Sv Stjepena (St Stephen's) dominates Hvar

Klis

Built on a narrow ridge of rock, with amazing views across Split and the coastal islands, the Tvrđava (Fortress) at Klis has often featured in Croatian history. Records show that there were Illyrian and Roman bulwarks here, but the castle really came to the fore as a principal holding of the first Croat state in the 7th century. It was a stronghold of the Uskoks (*see p81*) in the early 15th century, but fell to Muslim forces in 1537. From the impressive curtain walls and parapets, the Ottomans could look down menacingly on the Venetians who controlled Split, and watch the Adriatic Sea trade. In 1648 Venetian general Leonardo Foscolo mounted a full-scale attack and retook the fortress, causing much damage in the process.

Klis last saw 'active' service during World War II, when it was occupied by Italian and German troops.
12km (7½ miles) east of Split. Tourist information: Megdan 57.
Tel: (021) 240 578.
Tvrđava (Fortress), Klis. Tel: (021) 240 292. Open: Tue–Sun 9am–7pm, May–end Sept & Oct–Apr, Tue–Sun 9am–4pm. Admission fee.

Kornati Islands National Park
(*see pp139–40*)

Krka National Park (*see pp140–41*)

Makarska
Wedged between the Adriatic and the Biokovo Mountain, Makarska and its

The towering walls of the fortress at Klis rise high above Split

associated riviera is one of the best-established tourist areas in Croatia. The major draw is the long beach, now backed by large hotels. For attractions head to the Sv Filipa Nerija Samostan (St Philip's Monastery) with its medieval cloister, and the Franjevački Samostan (Franciscan Monastery) where you'll find the Malakološki muzej (Shell Museum), said to house one of the largest collections in the world. *42km (26 miles) south of Split. Tourist information: Obala Kralja Tomislava 16. Tel: (021) 612 002; www.makarska.hr*

Nin

Nin was declared capital of Croatia in the 7th century, soon after the Croats settled in the area. The town was built on a tiny island, connected to the mainland by a still extant stone bridge. Of the once-fine capital, little remains. However, it has the so-called 'smallest Cathedral in the world', Sv Križ (Church of the Holy Cross), which is currently being renovated. The town's Arheološki muzej (Archaeological Museum) has a fascinating collection of artefacts from these and earlier times including the re-creation of an early sailing craft. *20km (12½ miles) north of Zadar. Tourist information: Trg brać Radić 3. Tel: (023) 265 247; www.nin.hr*

Pag

Pag is a kind of 'love it or hate it' place. An island almost devoid of vegetation,

The Biokovo range rises dramatically behind the town of Makarska

its stark lunar landscape has a cheerless monotony for some and a surreal beauty for others, its bright white rock contrasting sharply with the azure waters immediately offshore. Though Pag isn't perhaps the holiday destination for everyone, it certainly offers a fascinating location for exploration, and is the heartland of two of Croatia's most renowned domestic products – sheep's cheese and lace.

Pag has been settled since ancient times, prized for the saltpans that lie in the Bay of Pag. The Romans founded a town here and, after the fall of the Roman empire, it was fought over by Venice and the Counts of nearby Zadar. Pag Town was sacked several times

because of this rivalry, but Venice won out in the end. They rebuilt the town according to a plan by Juraj Dalmatinac, who was also working on the Cathedral of St James at Šibenik (*see p82*) at the time. Work began in 1443. The town has been little altered in structure since then, although the walls have all but disappeared.

The second settlement on the island, Novalja, is the main tourist resort. It has a renowned party scene in the summer, when the main clubs in Zagreb move to open-air locations at Zrće Beach.

Sheep outnumber people many times over on Pag. The island is a patchwork of small stone pens designed to keep the animals warm and the flocks separated. Their cheese is prized throughout the country for its salty and herby taste. While the men were out on the waters seeking the next catch, the women watched the flocks and made lace. Over the years Pag lace became known as the finest in Croatia, and was also renowned throughout the Venetian and Austrian empires. A lace-maker from Pag was employed full time at the court of Empress Maria Theresa, to supply the royal needs. You can buy both cheese and lace at roadside stalls throughout the island.

50km (31 miles) north of Zadar. Tourist information: Od Špitala 2, Pag Town. Tel: (023) 611 286; www.pag-tourism.hr Pag is connected to the mainland at its southern tip, but there's a ferry to Pag town from Karlobag on the mainland.

Plitvice Lakes National Park (*see p143*)

Primošten

One of the longest-standing of the tourist resorts along the Dalmatian coast, the oldest part of Primošten is an island community, now linked to the mainland by a short bridge. Pretty whitewashed and stone houses compete for every inch of dry land and offer fascinating corners to explore. Above the rooftops, the church of St George looks down on the clear bay. The church guards a sacred icon of the Virgin.

Over the bridge on the mainland you'll find the modern trappings of tourism and a large marina. The lands around the town are famed for their Babić wines.

18km (11 miles) south of Šibenik.

Tourist information: Trg Biskupa Arnerića 2. Tel: (022) 571 111; www.summernet.hr

Salona

Capital of the Roman province of Dalmatia, Salona – or, to give the city its full name, Colonia Martia Iulia Salona – was one of the largest cities in the eastern Mediterranean. By the time Emperor Diocletian (*see pp92–3*) was born here in the mid-3rd century AD, it had a population of 60,000, with grand public buildings spread across a wide area of the coastal plain. In the later Roman and early Byzantine era, the city became an important centre of Christianity, hosting two synods in the 6th century before finally being abandoned with the arrival of the Croats in the 7th century.

Split and northern Dalmatia

Primošten perches on a rocky isthmus

Today, archaeologists have merely scratched the surface of the area: untold treasures must surely lie under the vineyards and vegetable fields that abut the extant remains. Sadly, the modern world has encroached on Salona's faded majesty, with Split's heavy industry in the near distance and the drone of its heavy traffic filling the air. Try to visit on Sundays, when there's bound to be less truck noise.

Many of the excavated remains date from the Christian era of Salona's history (mid-4th to late 6th century AD). The Manastirine complex next to the ticket office is the site of the burial of Bishop Domnio, executed by Diocletian in AD 304 during his most vehemently anti-Christian era. The site later became a Christian pilgrimage site. The basilica here dates from the mid-4th century, though it was rebuilt after Vandal attacks in the 7th century.

The Tusculum building, where tickets are sold, looks rather like a Victorian folly, with disparate bits of ornate Roman statuary and cornice thrown together to form a window frame or decorative panel. Still, it does show the fine work that once graced the buildings here, all of which has vanished to museums or elsewhere. South of the Tusculum lie the vast remains of the Thermae (Baths) and the Episcopal Centre, which was one of the most important centres of Christianity in the 6th century. You can also see sections of excellent road, now disappearing into farmland. West of the Episcopal complex, a partly paved road leads to Kapljuč (Basilica of the Five Martyrs), built on the burial site of the priest Asterius and four imperial guards, also executed in 304. Further west is the amphitheatre. Strong foundations and interior walls hint at what a fine building it would once have been.

Lovers of uncultivated ancient remains could spend many hours here, as there are many other buildings poking through the undergrowth just waiting to be explored.

5km (3 miles) west of Split.
Salona Archaeological Site, Put stare Salone, Solin. Tel: (021) 211 538.
Open: Mon–Fri 8am–7pm, Sat 10am–7pm, Sun 4–7pm.
Admission fee.

The Roman amphitheatre at Salona

Senj

The impressive Nehaj Castle dominates the high ground above this coastal town. It stood on the border between Hungarian and Ottoman territory, and was thus an important outpost of the Vojne Krajina (Military Frontier) – the string of fortifications that marked the boundary between the two empires. The fortress dates from the 1550s and now houses a museum devoted to the Uskoks, Christians who fled lands taken by the Muslim Ottomans. They continued to fight for their homelands but also became a thorn in the side of their Hungarian allies when they began attacking Venetian interests.

50km (31 miles) south of Rijeka.
Tourist information: Stara cesta 2.
Tel: (053) 881 068.

Šibenik

A thriving town until 1991, six days of intensive fighting here during the war brought devastation to the ports and damage to many historic buildings. Today, though, the old heart of Šibenik is a bustling place once again. It's more of a working town than a tourist town – the narrow streets crammed with the accoutrements of daily life, sitting happily alongside magnificent Gothic and Renaissance architecture – but it is still worth a trip to see.

Most people come to visit one building, the Katedrala Sv Jakova (Cathedral of St James). Its unique design – Gothic lower part and Renaissance roof and dome – captures the precise moment of the Gothic transformation into Renaissance. The cathedral was added to the UNESCO World Heritage list in 2000. The structure is worthy both for its design and its decoration. Started in 1431 under a Venetian, Francesco di Giacomo, much of the finest work is attributed to his successor Juraj Dalmatinac (see p23). It was continued in turn after his death in 1475 by Nikola Firentinac. After Firentinac's death in 1505 work continued until 1535. The stone barrel roof and dome by Firentinac were the first of their kind, and the stone sections are so finely worked that they fit together without mortar.

The church is also unique in that the interior dimensions exactly match the exterior; there is no ceiling vaulting or interior wall finish – what you see is the stone of the exterior walls. For much of the exterior decoration we have to thank Dalmatinac. He sculpted the 71 individual human faces forming a frieze above the windows, and the Door of the Lions, depicting two animals supporting Adam and Eve. The main doorway is a grand Gothic affair, showing images of the saints.

The Cathedral Square offers one of the finest ensembles of buildings in the city, including the 15th-century Bishop's Palace and High Renaissance-style Town Hall. The old loggia (16th century), once seat of the town council, faces the Door of the Lions, while behind it ornate façades of golden stone climb the hillside. Further up is the Fort of St Anne (also known as Sv Mikela or St Michele), which crowns the hill of the old town. The medieval castle suffered the ignominy of being destroyed when a bolt of lightning caused the arsenal to explode; the whole structure had to be rebuilt. You'll get excellent views across the old town – and out to the unsightly docks around the town – from here.

Ample evidence of the strong city walls remain, often decorated by plaques and reliefs depicting Sv Mihovil (St Michael), patron saint of the city. *82km (51 miles) north of Split. Tourist information: Obala Dr Franje Tuđmana 5. Tel: (022) 214 411; www.sibenik-tourism.hr Katedrala Sv Jakova (Cathedral of St James), Trg Republike Hrvastke 1. Tel: (022) 711 049. Open: May–Sept Mon–Sat 8.30am–8pm; Oct–Apr daily 8.20am–noon, 4–6.30pm.*

Sinj

Set inland on the road to Bosnia, the site of Sinj was settled by the Romans,

The roof and dome of Sv Jakova (St James's), Šibenik: a 15th-century architectural marvel but the town grew up later around the 15th-century Franjevački Samostan (Franciscan Monastery). Captured by the Turks in 1513, it remained under their control until taken by the Venetians in 1699. When the Ottomans attempted to retake the town again in 1715, the townsfolk rose up against them, achieving a victory still celebrated annually with Sinjska Alka, a jousting contest that takes place on the first weekend in August.

26km (16 miles) northeast of Split. Tourist information: Vrlicka 50. Tel: (021) 826 352; www.tzsinj.hr

Split

When, at the end of the 3rd century AD, Emperor Diocletian bought a prize patch of land on the coast just a few kilometres away from his hometown of Salona (*see pp79–80*), there was no other building in sight. He built himself a palace – a huge fortified enclave measuring 4,500sq m (48,438sq ft) – where he spent the last few years of his life in opulent retirement. It was one of the finest Roman structures in the Eastern Empire, with verdant gardens, temples and lavish living quarters.

In AD 615 Salona was attacked by pagan tribes, so the people took refuge in the palace compound (by then the governor's residence); in the years that followed they settled within its walls. This was the birth of the city of Split, now Croatia's second city after the capital Zagreb. Today, though much of the palace has been lost to history, tantalising elements can still be found. The main land entrance, Zlatna Vrata (Golden Gate), which is currently undergoing renovation, can still be seen, with the mainly 11th-century Sv Martin (St Martin's Church) behind it. The much plainer Broncana Vrata (Bronze Gate) – also known as Mjedena Vrata (Brass Gate) – on the seaward side and Željezna Vrata (Iron Gate) also still exist, the latter incorporated into the 11th-century Crckva Gospa od Zvonika (Church of Our Lady of the Belfry). The most obvious and romantic element of the palace is the peristyle, once an interior colonnaded courtyard and now a popular meeting place.

A view of Split and the mountains beyond

Mending fishing nets is a daily chore

The site of Diocletian's mausoleum is today's Katedrala Sv Dujma (Cathedral of St Domnius), consecrated in the 7th century. The Emperor's remains were removed and those of Duje, Bishop of Split, interred here. The bulk of the edifice is pure Byzantine, set on the original Roman ground plan. It even utilises the original Roman columns and friezes, including some depicting Diocletian himself. The interior decoration is later, including the 15th-century Altar of Domnius by Bonino of Milan, and the Altar of St Anastasius (1448) by Juraj Dalmatinac. The cathedral has a museum with liturgical treasures and valuable manuscripts.

Another carefully exploited Roman temple is that of Jupiter, now Sv Ivan Krstitelj (St John the Baptist), consecrated in the 6th century and containing the tombs of other bishops of Split. The modern statue of St John is by Ivan Meštrović.

Narodni Trg (People's Square) is t he modern-day heart of the old town, and abuts the site of the Palace. Here you will find some pleasing Gothic and Renaissance façades, including the Town Hall, which houses the Etnografski muzej (Ethnological Museum). Inside is a range of traditional costumes, crafts and tools.

Split has several other major museums. The Arheološki muzej (Archaeological Museum) houses an

An octopus drying in the Croatian sun

exceptional range of Roman artefacts from the palace and the site at Salona, plus important early Christian finds from the basilica complexes that developed here. The muzej Hrvatskih Arheoloških Spomenika (Museum of Croatian Archaeological Monuments) moves on to the later dates in the city's history, with outstanding Byzantine and Romanesque objects including much religious decoration. The muzej Grada Splita (Split Town Museum) concentrates on the civic development of the town from the medieval era to the 20th century, taking each era in turn. Staying in the 20th century, Split has an important collection of Ivan Meštrović's work dating from the time when he worked here during the 1930s. The Galerija Meštrović (Meštrović Gallery) is housed in a studio

designed by the sculptor himself and features pieces produced here. On the same ticket you can visit the 17th-century house (Šetalište Ivan Meštrovića 39), bought by Meštrović to use as gallery space.

Although metropolitan Split is now a very large, and often ugly, industrial city, its citizens benefit from the 'green lung' of Mount Marjan, a nature reserve bounded by the sea to the west of the city. It's a great place for picnicking, strolling or mountain biking.

198km (124 miles) north of Dubrovnik. Tourist information: Crešmirova. Tel: (021) 348 600; www.visitsplit.com
Arheološki muzej (Archaeological Museum), Zrinsko-Frankopanska 25. Tel: (021) 329 340. Open: 2 Oct–end May Tue–Fri 9am–2pm, Sat & Sun 9am–1pm; June–1 Oct Mon–Sat 9am–2pm, 4–8pm. Admission fee.
Etnografski muzej (Ethnological Museum), Narodni Trg 1. Tel: (021) 344 164. Open: mid-Sept–end May Mon–Fri 9am–2pm, Sat 9am–1pm; June Mon–Fri 9am–2pm & 5–8pm, Sat 9am–1pm; July–mid-Sept Mon–Fri 9am–9pm, Sat 9am–1pm & 6–9pm, Sun 10am–1pm. Admission fee.
Galerija Meštrović (Meštrović Gallery), Šetalište Ivan Meštrovića 46. Tel: (021) 340 800. Open: mid-May–end Sept Tue–Sun 9am–9pm; Oct–mid-May Tue–Sat 9am–4pm, Sun 10am–3pm.
Muzej Grada Splita (Split Town Museum), Papalićeva 1. Tel: (021) 341 240. Open: June–Sept Tue–Fri

9am–noon, 5–8pm, Sat & Sun
10am–noon; Oct–May Mon–Fri
10am–5pm, Sat & Sun 10am–noon.
Admission fee.
Muzej Hrvatskih Arheoloških Spomenika
(Museum of Croatian Archaeological
Monuments), Gunjačina b.b. Tel: (021)
358 420. Open: Tue–Sat 10am–1pm,
5–8pm, Sun 10am–1pm.

Trogir

Built on a tiny islet just 20m (65ft) off
the Dalmatian coast, and cushioned
from the bora wind by Čiovo island
just seaward of it, Trogir was a Venetian
stronghold that's now developed into
one of the prime yachting centres
of the Adriatic.

Contained within its watery
boundary, made impregnable by
impressive walls, Trogir old town is one
of the highlights of the Croatian coast;
exquisite architecture abounds, so that
even the most humble abode boasts
Gothic window frames or a Renaissance
portal. Unlike Zadar, with its orderly
grid of fine streets, Trogir is a confusing
maze of alleyways designed to foil
intruders. Now they serve simply to
frustrate the summer visitor, who is not
helped by the virtually useless map
issued by the tourist office.

The bulk of the important buildings
lies on the eastward side of the island.
Pride of place goes to Katedrala Sv
Lovre (Cathedral of St Lawrence) on

Time to relax after a day at sea

Split and northern Dalmatia

Trg Ivana Pavla II, which is a Romanesque masterpiece. The ornate main portal, carved *c*1240, is Master Radovan's *tour de force*. The portal was the subject of an intense renovation which was completed in June 2006. Arches and columns abound in images of the saints and biblical scenes, augmented by depictions of the activities during the 12 months of the year. Within the church, the Chapel of the Blessed Orsini (started 1468), housing the remains of the first Bishop of Trogir, is the highlight. It is ornately decorated with carvings of 12 saints by Nikola Firentinac and Andrija Aleši. The church bell tower dates from after the main building, and took so long to complete that each storey offers a different architectural style.

Trg Ivana Pavla II is completed by the 15th-century Gradska vijećnica (Town Hall) (original façade but modern interior), the 14th-century loggia and the simple clock tower, with reliefs sculpted by two Croatian masters of very different eras: Nikola Firentinac (1470) and Ivan Meštrović (1950).

Nikola Firentinac appears to have spent a good deal of his working life in Trogir. His work, a sculpture called *Deposition*, appears in the 13th-century Crkva Sv Ivan Krstitelja (Church of St John the Baptist), and he renovated Sv Dominik (St Dominic's), part of a 13th-century monastery complex, in the 16th century.

Among the array of secular architecture, be sure to study the façades of the Palača Čipiko (Čipiko

The Meštrović Mansion, now a gallery devoted to the sculptor

The towers of Trogir rise behind the high curtain walls on the waterfront

Palace), completed in the 1450s, and the Palača Stafileo (Stafileo Palace), built a couple of decades later, for their exceptional Gothic and Renaissance features. The Baroque Palača Garagnin-Fanfogna (Garagnin-Fanfogna Palace) houses the muzej Grada Trogira (Trogir Town Museum) if you want more details of Trogir's history. Perhaps one of the finest sights in the town is the wall of buildings flanking the southern boundary of the island, best viewed from across the bridge.

On the westward (seaward) flank of the island, surrounded by parkland, is Kula Kamerlengo (Kamerlengo Tower), the protective fortress of the town, begun in the 13th century and completed by the 1600s.

24km (15 miles) north of Split.
Tourist information: Gradska vijećnica
(Town Hall), Trg Ivana Pavla II/I.
Tel: (021) 881 412.
Katedrala Sv Lovre (Cathedral of St Lawrence) (Trg Ivana Pavla II)
Kula Kamerlengo (Kamerlengo Tower).
Open: mid-June–mid-Sept daily 9am–8pm; mid-Sept–mid-June 9am–sunset. Admission fee.
Muzej Grada Trogira (Trogir Town Museum), Gradska vrata 4. Tel: (021)

PEKA

Ispod peka is a traditional method of cooking stews. Meat and vegetables, plus a little stock, are placed in a round roasting tin and put on a hot surface – traditionally the bricks of the fireplace. The tray is covered with an iron dome, which has been preheated until it glows. The dome is then covered in hot ashes and the stew left until ready – a kind of medieval cross between slow cooking and pressure-cooking. The result? Delicious!

*881 406. Open: mid-June–mid-Sept daily
9am–9pm; mid-Sept–mid-June Mon–Sat
8am–2pm. Admission fee.*
*Palača Čipiko (Čipiko Palace),
ul Gradska.*
*Palača Stafileo (Stafileo Palace),
ul Matije Gupca.*

Zadar

Once the largest city fortress under
Venetian rule, and never taken by the
Ottomans, old Zadar still sits cosily

The Byzantine masterpiece of
St Donat's Church

within some remarkably intact curtain
walls. It is accessed by four gates, the
finest of which is the Venetian Land
Gate (1543) on the eastern flank. The
orderly grid of streets within offers a
fascinating melange of architecture
from Roman to Baroque, so take your
time and enjoy all the detail.

The most important building can be
found around the old Roman Forum
(1st century AD), where there are still a
few visible ancient remains in the form
of columns and foundation walls. Sv
Donata (St Donat's), founded in the 9th
century as the Church of the Holy
Trinity and renamed after the patron
saint of Zadar in the 15th century, is a
tour de force of early Byzantine
architecture. The narrow arched
windows and sombre styling are
brought to new heights by the circular
design. The interior is spartan, yet
incredibly beautiful for its lack of
ornate decoration. The building has
been deconsecrated and is now often
used as a concert venue.

Across the Forum from the church is
the Arheološki muzej (Archaeological
Museum), which takes you on a
chronological journey through Zadar's
history, with excellent pre-Classical
ceramics, ample Classical Roman
artefacts and a model of how the forum
would have looked in its heyday. It also
has later Byzantine and early Middle
Ages religious items.

The highest-ranking church in the
city is Katedrala sv Stošije (Cathedral of
St Anastasia), the largest Romanesque

church in Dalmatia. Its elegant façade is topped by a gallery of simple blind arches. The interior has a 5th-century floor mosaic, but the altars are flamboyant Baroque, contrasting sharply with the discreet exterior.

Amongst more than 15 other churches in the town, the highlights are Sv Šime (St Simeon's Church) and Franjevački Samostan i crkva sv Frane (Church Monastery of St Francis). St Simeon's safeguards the remains of St Simeon, whose body was brought here after a storm drove the boat carrying it to Venice into shelter at Zadar. The remains are contained in an ornate gilded silver casket (1381), a fine example of local craftsmanship for which Zadar was long famed. The Church Monastery of St Francis is the oldest Gothic church in Dalmatia.

One of the finest collections of religious art and liturgical objects, displayed as the Zlato I Srebro Zadra (The Silver and Gold of the City of Zadar), is found in the Convent of St Mary's. The collection includes objects from the 8th to the 18th centuries, recovered from churches throughout the town and regions around. The church was originally erected in 1066 but has undergone many alterations. The bell tower is Romanesque, dating from 1105.

In 2005 Zadar opened one of the country's most unusual attractions. The Sea Organ is part of a huge redevelopment of the Nova Riva waterfront and creates music from the natural movement of the incoming waves.

There are no large hotels in the old town itself. A modern resort has sprung up at Borik, just north of town, with a selection of large hotels and water-sports facilities.

75km (47 miles) north of Šibenik. Tourist information: Trg Ivana Pavla II. Tel: (021) 881 412; www.zadar.hr Arheološki muzej (Archaeological Museum), 3 Trg opatice Čike. Tel: (023) 250 542. Open: mid-June–mid-Sept Mon–Sat 9am–noon, 5–8pm, Sun 9am–noon; mid-Sept–mid-June Mon–Sat 9am–2pm. Admission fee. Sv Šime (St Simeon's Church), Trg Šime Budinica. Zlato I Srebro Zadra (The Silver and Gold of the City of Zadar), Trg Zeleni. Tel: (023) 250 496. Open: Apr–Sept Mon–Sat 10am–12.30pm & 6–8pm, Sun 10am–12.30pm; Oct–Mar Mon–Sat 10am–12.30am & 5–6.30pm. Admission fee.

THE ZADAR ARCHIPELAGO

A series of islands lying between the Dalmatian mainland and the Kornati Islands (*see pp139–40*), the Zadar archipelago offers 300 islands and islets to explore. Most are unpopulated; the remainder sometimes only have a few hundred permanent residents. There are few hotels, but these islands are great places for hiking or sailing and are well worth visiting, if only for a day or two. Dugi Otok is the largest at 125sq km (48sq miles), where the long beach at Telašćica is a particular draw. Tiny Iž enjoys some unusual festivities during the summer (*see p159*).

Emperor Diocletian

The reign of Gaius Aurelius Valerius Diocletianus proved to be one of the most interesting in the late Roman era. He brought to a decisive end what is now known as the 'Imperial Crisis', when the cult of the general and the rise in influence of the army had resulted in civil war and many short-lived rulers. He also divided political power within the empire; this would later result in a formal schism and the development of the Byzantine Orthodox Empire. But he is remembered with disdain by the Church for his brutal treatment of the early Christians.

Born c AD 245 on the Dalmatian coast to a very humble family, Diocletian was poorly educated as a child but used a career in the army to improve his own personal standing. He moved through many positions of influence, gaining the then Emperor's eye with his sound judgement and control.

In 284, after the death of Emperor Carus, the empire was split between his two young sons, Numerian and Carinus. When Numerian (new Emperor of the East) died soon after in mysterious circumstances, Diocletian – seen as a safe pair of hands – was declared his successor. In the following year the other son Carinus was killed in battle against Diocletian's forces and Diocletian assumed control of the whole empire.

Rome was awash with disparate armies, and Diocletian had to secure increasingly fragile borders. To quell the power of the generals he divided the army into two elements: the border guard, a relatively powerless arm, and the palace troops, who were under his own personal command.

Initially he reigned as a despotic monarch, but he realised that his lands were too big to control alone. He divided the empire in two. Each half was ruled by an Augustus (Diocletian himself in the East and his trusted lieutenant Maxianus Augustus in the West), backed up by second-ranking Caesars (Constantius in the West and Galarius in the East). Succession within the empire would henceforth be clear. When an Augustus died, he would be replaced by the appropriate Caesar, who would then appoint a new Caesar as his second-in-command.

Diocletian also bolstered the religious Imperial Cult, identifying himself with the Roman god Jupiter, and Maximus with Hercules. This may initially have been as a propaganda exercise to strengthen the image of the empire in the minds of his citizens, because he was at first tolerant of other religions. However, over the period of his rule, his policies grew increasingly severe. Even though it is thought that his wife and daughter were Christians, all faiths other than the Imperial Cult were banned in 303 and many prominent Christians were put brutally to death, including Archbishop Maurus of Poreč and Bishop Domnio of Salona. Many of these are now canonised, beatified or revered as martyrs.

Diocletian abdicated in May 305. Unusually for a Roman emperor, he was able to enjoy a few years of retirement, which he spent at his palace 4km (2$^{1}/_{2}$ miles) from Salona on the Bay of Aspalathos (now in the heart of Split). He died there in c313.

Diocletian's Palace in Split, one of the most important buildings on the Mediterranean coast

Walk: Split

From Diocletian to Meštrović, this is a stroll through the history of Split, leading you to many of the highlights of the central city, including its major museums. How long it takes really depends on your own interest in the collections within. Obviously the main interest lies in Diocletian's Palace and how the old town has developed ergonomically around it. There are lots of cafés for rest stops and restaurants for lunch, so you can watch the citizens of modern Split going about their business while you delve into their history.

Allow: 3 hours.

Start just outside the Golden Gate, the main entrance to Diocletian's Palace.

1 Zlatna Vrata (Golden Gate)

Currently undergoing renovations and hidden behind cotton hoardings, this is the most ornate of the entrances. In the small gardens just outside the walls is a large statue of Grgur Ninski by Ivan Meštrović. Ninski was Bishop of Nin in

Diocletian's Palace from the Peristil

the 10th century (*see p134*), and is a Croatian folk hero. Rub his toe for good luck.

Enter through the gate and walk straight ahead down the narrow medieval street. At the first major intersection, Dominsova/Papalićeva, notice on the left a splendid Gothic palace, now home to the Museum of Split. The entrance is down Papalićeva on the left.

2 Museum of Split

The museum highlights manuscripts, paintings and other details of Split life and the city's development from the 12th to the 18th century, while the building displays many transitional Gothic to Renaissance features.

Return to the intersection of the two routes and turn left (continuing seaward down Dioklecijanova). After another 100m (328ft) you'll reach a square with the tourist information office ahead to your left. This area was the heart of Diocletian's Palace.

3 Cathedral of St Domnius

Behind the tourist office is Diocletian's mausoleum, now the Cathedral of St Domnius. The Corinthian columns of the small circular building betray its Roman origins, though the interior has many later features. Around the cathedral is the peristyle, which serves as an open square for the old town.

From the entrance to the cathedral take a left and go down the steps.

4 Diocletian's Palace

Here you'll find the foundations and cellars of Diocletian's Palace (*see pp92–3*). Still in excellent condition, today they are part museum, part marketplace.

Return to the Peristil and turn left down Krešimirova to walk along to Narodni Trg, also known as Pjaca.

Renaissance balconies abound

5 Pjaca

This area marks the transition from the palace to the town. As you enter the square, look back behind you to see the remains of Diocletian's Iron Gate, now forming part of the structure of the Church of Our Lady of the Belfry. Pjaca was the heart of the medieval town and still features many fine Gothic and Renaissance façades. The Renaissance Town Hall now houses the Ethnographic Museum, featuring traditional handicrafts, domestic tools and other artefacts.

From the square, take Marulićeva down towards the seafront (as you enter the square from Krešimirova, this is an immediate left turn). You'll reach Trg Braće Radića wth the Marina Tower (all that's left of the old Venetian fortress), then break out onto the wide seafront promenade. Look to your left here for a good view of the south wall of Diocletian's Palace with its enclosed arcades.

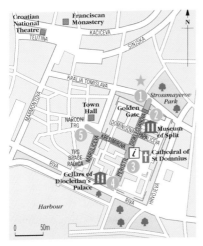

Driving tour: Hvar

The longest Adriatic island, with a length of almost 70km (44 miles), Hvar offers some interesting contrasts. Tourism plays an important economic role, but so too do winemaking, fishing and – most famously – lavender production. Although you can buy lavender products such as soap, pomanders and oils all year round, you'll need to make this tour during June to see the hectares of purple flowers at their best in the fields, and smell the scent in the air as you travel along. The island has been occupied since Neolithic times and was colonised by Greeks from the Aegean in the 4th century BC.

Distance: 80km (50 miles) one way. Allow: 6 hours.

1 Hvar Town

Begin your tour in the capital, Hvar Town, which is one of the finest medieval towns in the Aegean, and is overlooked by its castle. Wander the narrow streets of the old town before taking a stroll along the harbour promenade or visiting the Renaissance Katedrala Sv Stjepena (Cathedral of St Stephen) or the Franjevački Samostan (Franciscan Monastery).

From Hvar Town take the route northeast signposted Stari Grad (route 116). The road climbs over the hills out of the town and past a couple of traditional villages before heading through a long tunnel. It then winds down into Stari Grad.

2 Stari Grad

Stari Grad was the Greek Pharos, the most important settlement on the

Explore the steep walkways of Hvar Town

island for many centuries. It now plays a secondary role to Hvar Town (the status of capital was transferred under Venetian rule). However, the main vehicle ferry terminal to the island still stands just outside the town.

The town is most famed today for the Renaissance Palace of 16th-century writer Petar Hektorović, erected c1520, also known as Kaštel Trvdalj, which he used as a summer residence.

Return to the 116 and follow signs for Jelsa. After 5km (3 miles) turn left to the small settlement of Vrboska.

3 Vrboska

Set at the head of a narrow coastal inlet, Vrboska was seen as susceptible to Ottoman attacks, so in response the townsfolk built St Mary's Church during the 15th century, a rare example of a Renaissance fortified place of worship, little altered since that time. The later (16th-century) St Lawrence's Church contains paintings by renowned Venetian artists of their day. *From Vrboska return to the 116 for the short journey to Jelsa.*

4 Jelsa

Also at the head of an inlet, Jelsa's 14th-century church was fortified during the 16th century. The village's central square is Baroque, which is a contrast to other main squares on the island, and boasts a fine church façade – that of St John's.

Continuing east from Jelsa towards Sućuraj, Hvar Island becomes very sparsely populated and the land falls steeply down to the sea. Twelve

Tiny coves are tempting spots for a picnic

kilometres (7½ miles) after the village of Zastražišće, you can turn left down to the tiny settlement of Rt Zaraće in order to enjoy views of the coast. Otherwise it's on through Gdinj, Bogomilje and Selca to Sućuraj.

5 Sućuraj

On the easternmost tip of Hvar, Sućuraj seems a world away from the relatively bustling Hvar Town. It was founded in the 16th century, and the ruins of a Venetian castle tell us of its original purpose. Today it boasts a ferry connection to the mainland, and you can finish your tour here, taking the boat to Drvenik 12km (7½ miles) north of Gradec, or retracing your steps back to Hvar Town.

Bird-watching

With its exceptionally varied natural landscape, and numerous protected regions, Croatia is one of the richest countries in Europe in terms of bird life. In addition to its many native birds, the country lies on the direct route for many migratory species, which make a pit stop here between their seasonal African and European homes. A total of 275 species has been documented within Croatian borders, and spring or autumn is the best time to visit for the sheer variety.

On the coast

The myriad offshore islands make the perfect nesting ground for gulls and other sea birds – most of the outer islands are well out of the reach of most people, except for a few intrepid sailors. The Adriatic is a conduit for many migratory species.

Two coastal reserves are easy to find: the Palud Ornithological Reserve (*see pp145–6*), close to Rovinj, and the Vranska Jezera Ornithological Reserve (*see pp146*), south of Zadar. Another less accessible vantage point would be the coastal wetlands of the Neretva Delta south of Ploče, but you'll need to hire a boat from a local village to reach the habitat.

Here are a few species to look out for. Divers or *Gaviiformes* include Red, plentiful in summer plumage, and Black-throated, which are more common than the Red. Cory's are rare but they do breed on the outlying Dalmatian islands, as do Mediterranean Shearwater. Storm petrel are rarely seen from land but breed on the Dalmatian islands; Cormorants and Shags are common, Tufted Ducks are widespread.

Inland

The numerous inland marshes and river drainage basins offer an excellent opportunity to see waders and waterfowl. The basins act as a natural overflow if river levels rise, and their complicated flora and fauna (able to cope with both very wet and semi-wet conditions) have been lost in most other places in western Europe where the rivers are now managed by man.

The Kopacevo Marshes, located near Baranya between the Drava and Danube rivers, offer the 'twitcher' 275 species to search for, while the Plitvice Lakes National Park has 126 documented species, with 70 breeding species.

Searching for the close-up

Jelas Polje, on the route of the Sava River, downstream of Zagreb, has the largest colony of bitterns and herons in Croatia, plus more than 100 other nesting species and 230 species in total throughout the year. Two hundred and twelve species have been documented at Paklenica. The most interesting areas to explore are the Velika and Mala Paklenica canyons, where there is a small colony of Griffon Vultures. A qualified ornithologist leads either full- or half-day bird-watching tours for a fee.

Endemic wetland species include Great White Egret (common), Grey Heron (common), Capercaillie (rare) and Coot (common). Migratory species include Spoonbill, Glossy Ibis, Purple Heron (summer) and Greylag Goose (*Anser anser*).

Problems for the future

Surprisingly, the beacon of economic hope that the membership of the European Union brings has also posed a conundrum for the Danube and its numerous tributaries. It is one of the EU's core policies to facilitate and promote the use of environmentally friendly forms of transport. As part of this it aims to get cargoes onto the water if at all possible, and the Danube is seen as fundamental to this aim. However, the Navigation And Inland Waterway Action and Development in Europe (NAIADES) action plan, signed in January 2006, involves the elimination of what the EU calls 'strategic bottlenecks', some of which are the last unfettered sections of the Danube valley, causing irreparable damage to the remaining marshlands along the river's path. Environmentalists are up in arms at what they see as a blatant disregard for some of the last pristine river-drainage systems in Europe.

Useful organisations

The Royal Society for the Protection of Birds (RSPB) provides information and activities for bird-watchers, with affiliations to international organisations.

The Royal Society for the Protection of Birds (RSPB), The Lodge, Sandy, Beds, SG19 2DL, Tel: 01767 680551, www.rspb.org.uk
www.birdingpal.org puts birders around the world in touch with one another.

Dubrovnik and southern Dalmatia

The southernmost region of Croatia is a long slim strip of land hugging the Adriatic. Much is different here compared to the north – the days are longer and hotter and the lifestyle more languorous.

The region is anchored by Dubrovnik, this fortified old town, a gem of Renaissance architecture; but there is much more to southern Dalmatia than its *pièce de résistance*. You can see most of the area from a base in Dubrovnik itself, via ferry-boat trips or water-taxi. Here you can really let the water be your highway.

In the north of the region several islands are the draw – Korčula, with its gorgeous old town, and the tiny Elaphite Islands. Mljet Island is part National Park, or you can head to the Pelješac Peninsula for some of the best wines in the country. The Konavle region is Croatia's 'deep south'. Here the vegetation is almost Caribbeanesque: lush banana plants and palms sit side by side with deep magenta bougainvillea. The tiny bays around its main town, Cavtat, attract an upmarket Croatian and Italian crowd, making it one of the chicest places to be in the summer.

CAVTAT

Set in a lush bay in the far south of Dalmatia, Cavtat offers a genteel and picturesque location for lunch or dinner under the shade of swaying palms or colourful frangipani. There's nothing much to the town itself: the 15th-century church of St Blaise adorns the seafront, there's a 15th-century

Franciscan monastery, and the Renaissance Duke's Palace displays the Bogišić Collection of art, antiques and ethnographic items bequeathed by a local 19th-century philanthropist. However, it attracts the upmarket yachting crowd during the summer. Many visitors take a water-taxi or tour-boat from Dubrovnik (approx 30 mins) simply to enjoy the quieter atmosphere of Cavtat for a few hours.

There are several large resort hotels north and south of the town.
23km (14 miles) south of Dubrovnik. Tourist information: Tiha 3, Cavtat. Tel: (020) 479 025; www.tzcavtat-konlave.hr. Bogišić Collection, Obala Starčevića 1. Tel: (020) 478 556. Open: Mon–Fri 9am–1pm. Admission fee.

DUBROVNIK

It's been called the 'Jewel of the Eastern Adriatic', and that is no overstatement – Dubrovnik is unique and one of the world's 'must-see' cities.

One of the most important and influential settlements in Europe throughout the second millennium, Old Dubrovnik dates almost exclusively from after the earthquake of 1667, when the medieval town was consumed by the post-quake fire. Much of the domestic architecture is quite austere when compared to Hvar or Korčula towns; the houses combine, however, to offer a very pleasing whole. The public buildings proffer different, more elaborate, façades, with some exceptional workmanship by the finest craftsmen in the Venetian world. It was placed on the UNESCO World Heritage list in 1979.

Dubrovnik is easy to explore. Placa or Stradun is the main artery of the city, running from the Pile Gate in the west to the harbour in the east. From

Dubrovnik and southern Dalmatia

The lush landscape of Cavtat

here a grid of narrow lanes leads off north and south. Loža – the main square of the town – sits just behind the old harbour. Here you'll find Orlandov stup (Orlando's Column), dating from 1419, a symbol of the freedom of Ragusa (*see pp112–13*).

Dubrovnik: one of the richest city-states of the second millennium

The walls and fortifications

Some of the most complete fortifications in the world, and in parts up to 25m (82ft) in height, the fortress walls define the old town as they have done since they were first raised in the 10th century. Taking the 2km (1¼-mile) circuit of the city walls is the perfect way to start your trip. From these you will have exceptional views of the town's position, the sheltered harbour and the layout of the narrow streets within the walls.

The entrance to the town from the sea is oriented northeast. Protecting its approaches you'll find Tvrđava sv Ivana (St John's Fort), a semicircular structure that now houses the Pomorski muzej (Maritime Museum) and a small aquarium. At one time, a chain was stretched across the harbour from St John's to signify times when Ragusa was closed for business. On the westward (land approach), the walls are strung between the smaller Tvrđava Bokar (Fort Bokar) in the south and Tvrđava

Minčeta (Fort Minčeta) in the north. Minčeta is considered the most beautiful fortification and was designed by Michelozzo Michelozzi in 1461 and completed by local master Juraj Dalmatinac.

Just outside the city gates, and not part of the wall tour (yet very much part of the whole), are the 1580 Tvrđava Revelin (Fort Revelin), the youngest of Dubrovnik's phalanx of defences, and Tvrđava Lovrijenac (Fort Lawrence), built atop a rocky outcrop southwest of Fort Bokar and now used for concerts and other public performances.

The walls are cut by four gates. Gradska Vrata Pile (Pile Gate) is the main entry from the modern town (west). The inner gate was completed in 1460, but the outer fortifications and the drawbridge date from 1537. Above the archway, a statue of St Blaise, patron of the city, looks down on all who enter.

Akvarij (Aquarium). Tel: (020) 427 937.
Open: June–Sept daily 9am–8pm;
Oct–May Mon–Sat 9am–5pm.
Admission fee.
Pomorski muzej (Maritime Museum).
Tel: (020) 323 904. Open: Oct–Apr
Tue–Sun 9am–2pm; May–Sept Tue–Sun
9am–6pm. Admission fee.
Town walls, entrances at Pile Gate on Od
Pustijerne, south of the harbour, or Sv
Dominika, north of the harbour. Open:
Apr–May & Sept–end Oct 8am–6pm;
June–Aug 8am–7.30pm; Nov–Mar
10am–3pm. Admission fee. Audio tour
in English.

Secular architecture

Ragusa's power and influence
centred very much on its secular
administration, so it isn't surprising
that many of its important attractions

Stradun is the arterial route of Dubrovnik

are non-religious buildings. Chief
amongst these is the Knežev dvor
(Rector's Palace), seat of the city
council, and home to each of the
council leaders during their month-
long turns in power *(see p112)*. Built
originally in 1435, the palace has been
expanded and altered with work by
Michelozzi, Dalmatinac and Onofrio
della Cava; the capitals of the portico
columns demonstrate stunning
precision. Today the palace houses the
Dubrovački muzej (Dubrovnik
Museum), which has a range of
artefacts including paintings of
Dubrovnik scenes and Dubrovnik
dignitaries, furniture, coins from the
mint and thousands of other items,
large and small, to help you build a
picture of the city.

Where the Rector's Palace upheld
political power, Palaca Sponza (Sponza
Palace) allows us to delve into the
economic machinations of Dubrovnik.
Built between 1516 and 1522 in late
Gothic-early Renaissance style, this
palace – located just inside the walls
from the harbour – was originally the
Customs House, then became the city
Mint. Today it houses Povijesni arhiv
(the State Archives). These archives
contain one of the most complete
records of trading, real estate and
monetary life in Europe. Official
documents cover all eras except for
those lost in the earthquake.

Other relics speak of a more
mundane yet still vital aspect of daily
life in Dubrovnik. Velika Onofrijeva

Dubrovnik and southern Dalmatia

Fontana (Big Onofrio's Fountain), just inside the Pile Gate, opened in 1438 as part of a huge public undertaking to provide fresh water and more sanitary conditions for the townsfolk. Designed by della Cava, it is both beautiful and practical. At the harbour end of the Stradun is the smaller Mala Onofrijeva Fontana (Small Onofrio's Fountain) of the same year.

Beyond Fort Revelin was another important building related to health. The Lazareti (Quarantine) was built to house those who wished to enter the town. There they were kept until they were deemed to be free of disease. It is one of the earliest of its kind; building began in 1377.

Dubrovački muzej (Dubrovnik Museum), Knežev dvor 1. Tel: (020) 321 422. Open: daily 9am–6pm. Admission fee.

State Archives. Sponza-Povijesni arhiv (Sponza Palace and Historic Archives). Tel: (020) 321 032. Open: Sun–Fri 8am–3pm, Sat 8am–1pm. Free.

Religious treasures

Because of Ragusa's influence and its security, many religious orders established monasteries here, and the numerous churches offer us some breathtaking architecture, as well as treasures in oils and precious metals.

The Katedrala (Cathedral of the Assumption) is pure Baroque, with an extravagant exterior and numerous large paintings in the interior, including an *Assumption* attributed to Titian. The Treasury safeguards many important religious relics and liturgical items, including the 'arm of St Blaise', encased in a 12th-century silver-gilt case studded with precious stones and enamels. Crkva Sv Vlaha (Church of St Blaise) is dedicated to the city's patron

The peaceful cloister of the Dominican Monastery

saint. It too is Baroque, and contains a silver-gilt statue of the saint holding Dubrovnik in his hands.

Of the four religious communities that can be found within the walls, two are especially important, with fine buildings and religious collections. In the 13th century the Dominicans took up residence at Dominikanski Samostan (the Dominican Monastery) in the northeast quarter of the city close to the Ploče Gate, but the current building is Renaissance. It houses an unusual central crucifix, a fresco on the wall above the main altar painted by Paolo Veneziano.

The Monastery Museum has an excellent collection of art that has been attributed mainly to the Dubrovnik and Venetian schools from the 13th to the 17th centuries, including a rich polyptych, *The Baptism of Christ* by Lovro Dobričević, which dates from 1448.

The Franjevački Samostan (Franciscan Monastery) was founded in the early 14th century, but only the south portal remains of the original Gothic building. The cloisters at the rear offer some of the finest Romanesque features in southern Dalmatia, whilst the monastery pharmacy at the entrance has been in continuous operation since 1317.

The open-mindedness of the Ragusans is clear in that other religions were also free to worship here. In the Jewish quarter around ul Žudioska, founded in 1546, you'll find the oldest Sephardic synagogue in Europe; you'll also find the remains of a mosque on ul M Pracata.

Crkva Sv Vlaha (Church of St Blaise), Luža Square. Open: daily 8am–8pm.

Dominikanski Samostan (Dominican Monastery), Sv Dominika. Tel: (020) 321 432. Museum open: daily 9am–6pm. Admission fee.

Franciscan Monastery, Stradun, just inside the Pile Gate. Tel: (020) 321 410. Museum open: 9am–6pm. Admission fee.

Katedrala (Cathedral of the Assumption), Poljana M. Držića. Tel: (020) 323 459. Open: June–Sept Mon–Sat 8am–8pm, Sun 11am–8pm, Oct–May Mon–Sat 8am–5.30pm, Sun

THE CONSEQUENCES OF WAR

From November 1991 until May 1992, the historic district of Dubrovnik received daily bombardment by the Yugoslav Federal Army, positioned on the high ground to the east. About 2,000 shells fell on the city; the Director of the Institute for Restoration's assessment was that 70 per cent of the buildings in the old city had been damaged during the siege. The estimated cost of restoring the city turned out to be astronomical, so some compromises had to be made: whereas fine Korčula stone had originally been used in constructing the city, now only the most important buildings were repaired using this. The rest was taken from a different source at Brač. Many countries donated money, as well as skilled masons and other artisans, who set about the gargantuan task of rebuilding the war-ravaged city, which amazingly has now almost been completed.

For evocative views of Dubrovnik at war, visit War Photo Limited, the gallery at Antuninska 6. Tel: (020) 367 467; www.warphotoltd.com

Dubrovnik and southern Dalmatia

Dubrovnik and southern Dalmatia

Korčula: a gem of Venetian town planning

11am–5.30pm. Admission fee. The
Treasury. (020) 411 715. Open: Mon–Sat
8am–5.30pm, Sun 11am–5.30pm.
Admission fee.
Synagogue, Žudioska 5. Tel: (020) 321
028. Open: June–Sept Mon–Fri
10am–8pm; Oct–May Mon–Fri
10am–1pm.

LOKRUM

Seven hundred metres (2,300ft) from
Dubrovnik is a small island, once home
to a Benedictine abbey, and later a
French fort and a Habsburg Palace. It is
now a nature reserve. Take one of the
taxi-boats from the harbour to enjoy
the forested pathways.
225km (140 miles) south of Split. Tourist
information: Dr Ante Starčevića 7. Tel:
(020) 427 591. Also on Stradun. Tel:
(020) 321 561 (but this office often has
less information); www.dubrovnik-
online.com

ELAFITSKI OTOCI
(The Elaphite Islands)

Lying offshore just to the north of
Dubrovnik, this small group of islands
was a popular place for Ragusan nobles
to spend the summer. They built lavish
villas here in which they could relax.
Today the three populated islands,
Šipan, Lopud and Koločep, renowned
for their beaches and quiet bays, are
popular destinations for day-trippers
taking boats from Dubrovnik.

Koločep is the closest to Dubrovnik.
It was Ragusan territory from the
9th century and has many patrician
mansions. In Donje Čelo the remains
of a fort watch over the Gothic chapel
of St Anthony, while an earlier
12th-century church in Gorne Čelo is
also dedicated to the saint.

Šipan is the largest island, known for
its olives and grapes. There are several
settlements here. Visit Suđurađ to see
some fine Renaissance houses and the
ruins of the Bishop's Palace, and
Šipanski Luka for the early Christian St
Michael's Church.

Lopud's only town, also called Lopud,
has a late 15th-century church, Sv
Marija od Spilica (St Mary of Spilica),
with fine Renaissance paintings and
16th-century cloisters.

In addition, the ruins of two forts
now stand guard over the town.
10km (6 miles) north of Dubrovnik.
Tourist information: Šipan – Šipanska
luka. Tel: (020) 758 084. Lupod – Radno
vrijeme. Tel: (020) 759 086. Ferries and
boat trips from Dubrovnik.

GRADAC

Lying equidistant between Split and Dubrovnik, Gradac is a growing tourist resort. It is popular for its beach, which it boasts is the longest in Croatia, a pale ribbon of shingle lapped by the azure Adriatic that runs for about 5km (3 miles) around several bays.

130km (81 miles) north of Dubrovnik. Tourist information: Stjepana Radića 1. Tel: (021) 697 511.

KORČULA

Named by the Greeks for the Black Forests (Korkyra Malaina) of holm oak that blanketed the interior, Korčula has long been one of the most prized islands of the Adriatic. For centuries shipbuilding was a major source of income (the trees produce long, sturdy wooden planks). Meanwhile the stone quarried at Vrnik was used in the building of many of the best Venetian and Ragusa (Dubrovnik) palaces – and in the 6th century, when Korčula belonged to the Byzantines, it was even shipped to Constantinople (now Istanbul) to be used in the fabric of Ayia Sofia Church. The famous explorer Marco Polo was born here in 1254, in the capital Korčula Town, a diminutive yet exquisite example of a Venetian settlement. Set on a tiny peninsula and still completely surrounded by thick, 13th-century walls, the main streets rise up to a small central square crowned by the Katedrala Sv Marko (Cathedral of St Mark), which has exceptional Gothic detail and an elaborate rose window.

The interior contains *St Mark with St Jerome and St Bartholomew* by Tintoretto and a Meštrović statue of St Blaise. Next door, the Opatska Riznica (Abbey Treasury) has a small but quality collection of art including examples attributed to Titian, Veronese and Bellini. Across from this is the Gradski muzej (Town Museum), housed in the Renaissance Gabriellis Palace, which traces the development of the city.

As an island once peopled by master stonecutters and rich merchants, it isn't surprising to find ornate decoration on just about every house and mansion.

The old main entrance to the town is also a *tour de force*, Kopnena vrata erected in 1391. This once guarded the

One of Korčula's historic towers

narrow canal that separated the town from the mainland. Today a sweeping Baroque staircase allows pedestrian entry, and another of the same period allows entry from the quayside to the south. The house of the young Marco Polo has recently been renovated and holds an exhibition about the explorer's life.

Korčula Island provides many more delights for tourists, particularly its lush landscape. In the centre is Blato, one of the largest towns, where the remains of the Roman Tonum Junianum villa have been found. The Renaissance/Baroque Arnerić Palace, once home to the noble Arnerić family, houses artefacts found there. Blato parish church, Sv Sveti (All Saints), safeguards the remains of St Vincenza, patron of the town, who is commemorated in a colourful festival on 28 April (*see p108*).

KORČULA FESTIVALS

Korčula Town is known for its 'Moreška' festival, which dates back hundreds of years. The Moreška and Kumpanjija are colourful and dynamic 'fighting dances', commemorating the battle between Christians and Moors that is said to have ensued when the Muslims kidnapped a girl from Korčula. Today they are stylised battles of good against evil in which evil must always be defeated.

There are festivals with sword dances throughout the island. The authentic Moreška performance takes place on 29 July, while related authentic Kumpanjija sword dances are performed in Blato on 28 April, in Pupnat on 5 August and in Smokvica on Assumption Day, But the dances are re-enacted for tourists throughout the summer season.

As you travel you'll pass numerous vineyards. These produce wines and stronger drinks, including *lozovaća* (cognac-style rakia), *travarica* (rakia with herbs) and *grk* (a sweet digestive).
5km (3 miles) southwest of the Pelješac Peninsula.
Ferry connections with Rijeka, Split, Hvar, Dubrovnik and Orebić.
Gradski muzej (Town Museum), Trg sv Marka. Tel: (020) 711 420. Open: mid-July–end-Aug daily 9am–9pm; May–mid-July & Sept–Oct daily 9am–1pm by prior appointment for groups only. Admission fee.
Opatska Riznica (Abbey Treasury), Trg sv Marka. Tel: (091) 559 7604. Open: mid-July–end Aug daily 9am–9pm; May–mid-July & Sept–Oct daily 9am–3pm. Admission fee.
Tourist information: Obala Franjo Tuđmana 1. Tel: (020) 715 701.

LASTOVO

The largest island of the Korčula Archipelago (a group of around 40 or so islets), Lastovo is a barren karst island rich in fragrant *macchia* (wild herbs and scrub). The island was the domain of the Yugoslav military during the communist era. Lastovo belonged to Ragusa (Dubrovnik) from the late 13th century, and Lastovo Town has a number of fine Gothic and Renaissance buildings.
20km (12½ miles) south of Korčula.
Tourist information: 20290 Lastovo. Tel: (020) 801 018; www.lastovo-tz.net
Ferry connections from Vela Luka on Korčula.

MLJET (*see p141*)

NEUM

A narrow corridor of land splits the Croatian territory of the Dalmatian coast. This tiny strip of land, less than 10km (6 miles) wide, belongs to Bosnia-Herzegovina and is its only access to the sea.

Historically there has been a bridgehead here since an agreement between Ragusa and the Ottomans, when the Ottomans were given a stretch of coastal land to act as a buffer between Ragusa and the Venetians further up the coast. Neum is the only

BETTER BE SURE

If you are travelling in your own vehicle or in a rental car, make sure that you have insurance cover to transit the Neum corridor. If not, then you'll need to use the ferry service from Ploče (*see p111*) to Trpanj on the Pelješac Peninsula. This route will allow you to continue your journey without entering Bosnia-Herzegovinian territory. A bridge to the Pelješac is currently at the planning stage.

settlement here, a small summer resort with a large hotel complex. Most traffic makes the short transit to southern Croatia without stopping.
73km (46 miles) north of Dubrovnik.

Dubrovnik and southern Dalmatia

Enjoying a day trip around the islands

PELJEŠAC PENINSULA

Famed for its fine wines, the peninsula cuts northwest from the Dalmatian mainland just south of the Neum 'gap'. It's the largest in Dalmatia, with a length of 62km (39 miles). Wine-tasting and lunching on delicious oysters is the main activity here. Large oyster beds are set in the shallow Malostonski Kanal between the east coast of the peninsula and the mainland.

Pelješac was owned by Ragusa (Dubrovnik) from the 12th century until the fall of the Republic (1808). It formed a key 'outer' colony for the city, it provided Ragusa with some of the finest and world-renowned seafarers of the age, and it was an important source of salt from the pans in the coastal shallows in the south.

Ston is a fascinating place. Sitting on the narrow isthmus that connects Pelješac with the mainland, its 14–16th-century walls are one of the marvels of Dalmatian fortification. Five kilometres (3 miles) in length, with 41 towers and two main forts, they stretch over the hill to completely protect and control entry to the peninsula.

Two communities – Mali Ston on the east side of the hill and Veliki Ston on the west – make up Ston, and both were founded in 1333. Veliki Ston was the main area of settlement, with some fine palaces within its walls, including the Knežev Dvor (Governor's Palace) and the palaces of the Sorkočević and Đorđić families.

Mali Ston is the smaller and is now a rather sleepy place. With storage warehouses along the waterfront and a small grid of streets behind, it was guarded by Fort Koruna on higher ground above.

In the north of the peninsula, the main town, Orebić, is the jumping-off point for ferries to Korčula. It has an

Pelješac Peninsula stretches northwest from the Dalmatian coast

interesting Pomorski muzej (Maritime Museum) showcasing the lives of the mariners whose skills were so much in demand during the era of sail, and a large Franjevački Samostan (Franciscan Monastery) whose church contains a *Virgin with Child* by Nikola Firentinac.

The start of the peninsula is 68km (42½ miles) north of Dubrovnik.

Tourist information, Pelješka Cesta, Ston. Tel: (020) 754 452; www.tzo-ston.hr.

Also at Trg Mimbeli Orebić. Tel: (020) 713 718; www.tz-orebic.com.

Franjevački Samostan (Franciscan Monastery). Tel: (020) 713 007. Open: Mon–Sat 9am–noon, Sun 4–6pm. Admission fee.

Pomorski muzej (Maritime Museum), Trg Mimbeli. Tel: (020) 713 009. Open: Mon–Fri 8am–noon & 5–8pm. Admission fee.

PLOČE

Not an interesting place in itself, Ploče wasn't even founded until after World War II. However, south of the town lies the delta of the Neretva River, which offers a fascinating and unique region that was actually forged by humans. The delta has been partially drained to create a maze of small plots of land interspersed by waterways, a veritable market garden with crops being sold at the roadside as they come into season. The main town, Opuzen, built around a Venetian fortress, sits on the banks of the river. A nature reserve has been designated where the delta meets the

sea, and vast swathes of reed beds provide habitat for wading birds; these are best seen from the small settlement of Blace.

120km (75 miles) north of Dubrovnik. No tourist information.

TRSTENO

In the past rich patrician families from Ragusa built themselves lavish summerhouses up and down the coast; Trsteno was the retreat chosen by the Gučetić family. Today it is home to the finest gardens in southern Dalmatia. The villa was first erected in 1494 by Ivan Marinov Gučetić-Gozze, who also laid out the first gardens and planted the arboretum with many of the exotic plants being brought back from all corners of the globe by Venetian and Ottoman traders.

The original villa was destroyed in the 1667 earthquake, with the extant Renaissance building taking its place. Today it is surrounded by 25 hectares (62 acres) of gardens, including the original Gučetić garden, a neo-Romantic 19th-century garden, a historic olive grove, indigenous Aleppo pine and downy-oak forest, as well as *macchia* scrubland. There are approximately 100 families of plants, including Asian, Mediterranean and American varieties.

15km (9 miles) north of Dubrovnik. No tourist information.

Trsteno Gardens. Tel: (020) 751 019. Open: summer, daily 9am–7pm; winter, daily 9am–5pm. Admission fee.

From Ragusa to the Republic of Dubrovnik

One of the most influential and successful of the Mediterranean city-states, Ragusa rose in power from the late 14th century but flourished between the 15th and 18th centuries.

From the 7th century onward the city had consolidated its position under the patronage of Constantinople, then Venice, until in 1358 it came under nominal Croatian-Hungarian control. In 1382 Ragusa declared itself a free state, but it was never powerful enough to defend itself militarily. Instead it kept its autonomy by using the Venetian template of avoiding confrontation and instead employing astute diplomacy and the payment of tribute to the leading power or powers of the day.

Within Ragusa, control was concentrated in the hands of the patrician families, or *nobile*, but their administration was extremely forward-thinking. In 1377 the first quarantine system in the world was introduced; slavery was abolished as early as 1418; in 1434 a home for orphans was opened, and an aqueduct brought fresh water to the city in 1436. In foreign policy they were extremely successful. At one time there were almost 100 Ragusan consuls around Europe. All male *nobile* over the age of majority had to serve as members on the Great Council, and each member of the Great Council had to serve one month as Rector of the Republic – in turn, so that no individual or family could exert too much influence.

It was a city of trade but also of master shipbuilders. The Ragusa style of ship, the argosy, was respected around the known world, and the Ragusan flag – with the word '*Libertas*' emblazoned across it – expressed the sentiments of the whole population. The state had a fleet of more than 300 trading ships by the 16th century, and all trade was recorded and codified.

Strong defensive walls protected the city

Knezev dvor, the political heart of Ragusa

in the republic, when the arts and sciences flourished.

The halcyon days came to an abrupt end in April 1667, when a huge earthquake ripped the heart out of the city. Only 3,000 people are estimated to have survived, and although the city was rebuilt in fine style, it never fully recovered economically. Profits continued to decline as the Islamic empire decayed throughout the 1700s, though trading ships were still sailing as far afield as the United States as late as the 1780s.

Dubrovnik retained its political independence until 1806, when Napoleon's forces laid siege to the city walls. After holding out for a month, the population capitulated. In 1808 the Great Council was abolished and the city was amalgamated into the Illyrian States, the short-lived, French-backed, independent Slav 'country'.

Napoleon's final defeat brought a new world order. Instead of reinstating its independence, the Congress of Vienna recognised that the days of the city-state were over, and Dubrovnik was brought into Dalmatia under full Habsburg control. The city became an economic backwater, left behind as the tide of history swung away from the Adriatic, until it was 'reconquered' by an army of tourists in the late 20th century.

As Venice declined (*see pp28–9*), so the fortunes of Ragusa rose. In the 15th century it became known as the Republic of Dubrovnik, adopting its Slavic name. The city did not join in the anti-Ottoman actions carried out by other western northern European powers, so it never became a target for the Ottoman attacks that laid waste to cities like Rhodes.

In 1526 Dubrovnik acknowledged the Turkish sultanate, agreeing to pay tribute to Istanbul. Dubrovnik merchants traded with the Ottomans, being one of the few conduits for luxury goods from the Arab world. This was the zenith of cultural activity

Walk: Dubrovnik

Dubrovnik is a small city, yet full of historic attractions. This route links the major sites – perfect if you are on a whistle-stop tour, or want to see the main attractions before enjoying the atmosphere of the side streets at your leisure.

Allow: 3 hours.

Start at Pile Gate, the main land entrance into the walled town. This is a double-gated entrance. If you turn left down the ramp between the two gates, you'll see a plaque with a display showing where the shells fell onto the town during the 1991 bombardment. Once through into the city proper, you will enter a small square, from where it's possible to start a walk of the city walls (*see pp101–2*).

1 Poljana Paska Miličevića

On your right you'll see Big Onofrio's Fountain, which has been bringing fresh water into the town since 1438. To the left is St Saviour's Church, dating from 1520, and the entrance to the Franciscan Monastery (*see p105*) beyond St Saviour's. The pharmacy of the Franciscan complex has been in continuous use since 1317 (though of course it has had to be renovated regularly).
Return to the square and turn left to walk down Stradun (also known as

Placa), the arterial street of old Dubrovnik. At the end of Stradun you'll reach another small square, Loža.

2 Loža

At the centre of the square is Orlando's Pillar, a symbol of the Republic's freedom, dating from 1419. To the right is the Baroque Church of St Blaise (*see p104*), dedicated to the patron saint of the city, whilst to the far left you'll see the delicate portico of Sponza Palace (*see p103*), begun in 1516. This was the economic powerhouse of the Republic, where records of all transactions and

The Baroque Cathedral of the Assumption

trading agreements were made.
*Exit the square on the side opposite
Stradun, and take the gate through the
city walls.*

3 Old Port

Exit at the Old Port, where the city
trading fleet would dock. Today small
ferries and taxi-boats ply their trade
here, with trips out to Lokrum, Cavtat
and the Elaphite Islands.
*Return to Loža and take an immediate
right along Sv Dominika, keeping the city
walls to your right. The church of San
Sebastian will appear on the left and
behind this is the Dominican Monastery.*

4 Dominican Monastery

The 14th-century Dominican
Monastery (*see p105*) has one of the
finest treasuries of religious art and
liturgical artefacts in Croatia.
*From the monastery, walk back to Loža
and take the route directly ahead (Pred
Dvor). You'll walk past Little Onofrio's*

Testing the water at Big Onofrio's Fountain

*Fountain and the theatre on your left,
after which you'll reach the Rector's
Palace (see p103).*

5 Rector's Palace

Seat of political power during the
Ragusa Republic, the quality of the
masonry here reflected the wealth of
15th-century Ragusa. The Rector's
Palace is now home to the Dubrovnik
Museum, the perfect place to
glean background information
on the city.
Cross the street to the Cathedral.

6 Cathedral of
the Assumption

Built in Baroque style after
the previous edifice was lost
in the earthquake of 1667, the
Cathedral of the Assumption
(*see p104*) has a worthy
interior, including an
Assumption by Titian.

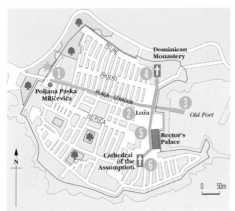

Drive: From Dubrovnik to the Pelješac Peninsula – the lands of the Ragusa Republic

Though immense in influence, Ragusa was diminutive in size. This tour takes you across the territory, exploring some of the factors that contributed to its success.

Distance: 200km (125 miles).

Allow: 5 hours.

Depart from Dubrovnik old town by following signs for Split. This will lead you up above the walls of the old town and through the new suburbs until you meet the Jadranska Magistrala main coastal road. Turn left here and travel through the villages of Zaton and Orašac until you reach Trsteno.

1 Trsteno
Here you'll find the summer palace of the Gučetić *nobile* family from Ragusa.

Fortifications at Mali Ston

Today it has the finest gardens in southern Dalmatia.
Continue on your journey northwest. The road offers splendid views of the Elaphite Islands just offshore as it hugs the coast around Luka Slano with its tiny village. Fifteen kilometres (9 miles) on from Slano you'll reach Zaton Doli. Take the left turn marked Ston.

2 Malostonski Kanal
The road runs along the eastern coastline here, giving you excellent views of the vast mussel and oyster beds seeded in the Malostonski Kanal, sheltered waters lying between the mainland and the peninsula. The shellfish are a speciality of the area and renowned throughout Croatia.
Five kilometres (3 miles) from the turn-off you'll reach Mali Ston.

3 Mali Ston
The eastern flank of one of the most fascinating fortifications in Europe, and founded in 1333, Mali Ston provided

practical support for the Ston defensive system, with vast storage warehouses on the quaysides (now hosting some excellent restaurants). Fort Kuruna stands proud above the hamlet.

From Mali Ston the road cuts directly west in the lee of Prevlaka hill. After 1km (about half a mile) you'll reach Veliki Ston.

Drive: From Dubrovnik to the Pelješac Peninsula

4 Veliki Ston

Veliki Ston is the larger of the two settlements. This was the residential quarters and administrative centre for Ston, and has some fine Renaissance palaces and strong fortifications.

Drive over the narrow bridge following signs for Orebić and Korčula, but pull over just beyond and look west.

5 The salt flats

The salt flats you see here were the reason for the economic success of Pelješac. Worked since Roman times, the flats are still in use today.

Continue in the direction Orebić/Korčula and head onto the Pelješac Peninsula proper. The road leads southwest, then cuts northwest up through the interior, past small vineyards set in the sheltered lees. The wines of this region are considered the best in Croatia, and several cooperatives offer tasting and buying. Twenty-seven kilometres (17 miles) from Ston the road hits the coast again at Drače (more mussel beds here) before turning inland then north towards

Orebić. Seventeen kilometres (10½ miles) north of Drače there's a right turn to the village of Trpanj and its ferry connection to the mainland. However, we'll carry on to Orebić.

6 Orebić

Famed for its seafarers, Orebić supplied Dubrovnik with its finest captains and navigators. The small museum in town is devoted to them and ancient trade routes and navigational methods, and there's a Franciscan monastery just inland.

Orebić has a regular 15-minute ferry (passenger and vehicle) service to Korčula. A visit here would be an excellent way to extend your tour.

A stall selling mussels and oysters on the Malostonski Kanal

Eastern Croatia

The swathe of land south and east of Zagreb and encompassing the regions of Baranja and Slavonia is the heartland of Croatian agriculture. A long, featureless plain all the way to the Danube, it comprises hectare after hectare of maize, apple orchards and fields of contented cattle, punctuated by somnolent river deltas that offer some of the country's most unspoilt wild landscapes.

The borders of the east encompass a finger of Croatian land that has been fought over since the fall of Rome. It was Slav territory, then the location of the *Vojne Karjine*, or Military Frontier, the Habsburg military border with the Ottoman Empire. When hostilities broke out in 1991 the eastern border region of Slavonia suffered the brunt of the Serb and Yugoslav bombardment, and was occupied for four years. The last Serb forces left in 1995, but the east wasn't returned to Croatian control until 1998. Though on the surface life has returned to normal, shattered buildings show that it is still early days. International help has been slower to arrive here than in other parts of the

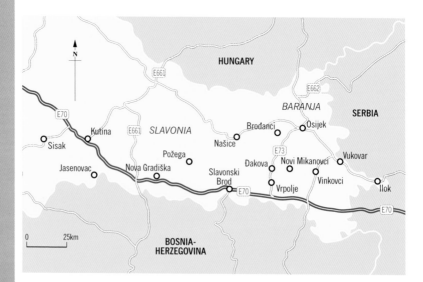

country, and it may be some time before the Danube corridor can truly call itself a tourist destination.

Brođanci

This tiny village is renowned for its 'Olympics of Ancient Sports', held during August, when the traditional sports of the region are brought together in one competitive 'meet'. A large fair has grown up around the competition, with handicrafts and food stalls.

25km (15½ miles) southwest of Osijek. No tourist information.

The red-brick Cathedral of St Peter at Đakova

Đakova

Đakova was a powerful bishopric from the 13th century, being the leading see of Slavonia until it was taken by the Turks.

The town is dominated by the massive red-brick, copper-domed Katedrala Sv Petar (Cathedral of St Peter), finished in 1882 as part of a wholesale urban redevelopment in the wake of the Ottoman withdrawal. Josip Strossmayer, who was bishop of Đakova at the time, brought in leading architects from Vienna to create a more-than-fitting main church. The façade is the most impressive element, with two 85m (279ft) bell towers. These dwarf the ornate but comparatively pocket-sized cupola.

38km (24 miles) south of Osijek. Tourist information: Kralja Tomislava 3. Tel: (031) 812 319.

Katedrala Sv Petar (Cathedral of St Peter), Trg Strossmayerovo. Tel: (031) 802 225. Open: daily 6am–8pm.

BISHOP JOSIP STROSSMAYER

Josip Strossmayer, who was born in Osijek, was committed to the pan-Slav culture, which was growing in influence throughout the region after the collapse of Ottoman control across the Balkans. He helped with the preparation and distribution of native language literature, while his interest in religious art is evident in the works that form the core of the collection in the Strossmayer Gallery of Old Masters in Zagreb (*see pp43–4*).

Ilok

Set on the Danube, this town – the easternmost in Croatia – has been fortified since the Middle Ages, after it became the domain of the counts of Ilok. Within the walls, the Franciscan monastery was erected on the spot where Ivan Kapistran, Franciscan monk and warrior, was buried in the 1450s.

In the early 1680s, the town was gifted to Livio Odescalchi, a Habsburg military chief, following his successful repulsing of the Ottomans. In 1683 he erected a three-storey Renaissance mansion, which hosts a number of attractions including a collection of Odescalchi family heirlooms.

39km (24 miles) southeast of Vukovar.
Tourist information: Trg Nikole Ilockog 2. Tel: (032) 590 020.
Monastery of St Ivan Kapistran.
Fra Bernadina Lejakovića 13.
For details of how to visit, contact the tourist office.

Jasenovac

Site of one of the Balkan's most notorious concentration camps, the largest built on Croatian soil during World War II, Jasenovac now plays host to an immense modern monument dedicated to the hundreds of thousands of Serbs, Jews and Roma (gypsies) who died here between 1941 and 1945. Nothing of the camp remains, but there is an education centre on the site.

50km (31 miles) west of Nova Gradiška.
Tourist information: Trg kralja Petra Svačića 3. Tel: (044) 672 490.

Kopački Rit Nature Park (*see p144*)

Kutina

The Erdödy family were feudal overlords of Kutina for many centuries.

They funded the erection of one of the finest Baroque churches in Croatia, Sv Marija Snježne (Church of Our Lady of the Snows) in the 1770s. The interior decoration is superb, with fine ceiling and wall frescoes and a blanket of painted stucco, but the wooden altar surround is a unique creation that is of most interest to scholars. The exterior portico is also unusual.

Neo-Gothic Erdödy Castle replaced an early family home and now houses the muzej Moslavine (Museum of Moslavina), which offers lots of background about the Moslavina region surrounding the town and displays local traditional costumes.

75km (47 miles) east of Zagreb.
Tourist information: Hvatskih branitelja 2. Tel: (044) 681 004.
Muzej Moslavine (Museum of Moslavina), Trg kralja Tomislava 13. Tel: (044) 683 569. Open: Tue–Fri 8am–1pm.

Lonjsko Polje Nature Park (*see p144*)

Našice

Feudal domain of the counts of Ilok (*see p119*), Našice is dominated by a large Franciscan monastery established in the early 14th century. The Baroque tower of their Sv Antun Padovanski (St Anthony of Padua) Church stands sentinel over the complex.

The town's Gradski muzej (Municipal Museum) is housed in a grand mansion built in 1811, once the home of musician and composer Dora Pejačević, which is surrounded by an English-style garden. The garden contains another villa built as a homage to the Sanssouci, the Rococo palace in Potsdam, Germany, that was designed by Frederick II of Prussia and completed in 1747.

55km (34½ miles) west of Osijek. Tourist office, Pejačevićev trg 4.
Tel: (031) 614 951; www.tznasice.hr
Gradski muzej (Municipal Museum), Pejačevićev trg 5. Tel: (034) 313 414.
Open: Mon–Tue 8am–3pm, Wed–Fri 8am–6pm, Sat 9am–noon.
Admission fee.

View of the main square in Nova Gradiška

80km (50 miles) west of Slavonski Brod.
Tourist information: Slavonski graničara 15. Tel: (035) 361 494; www.tzgng.hr

Nova Gradiška

Founded around a fort dating from 1725, the design of Nova Gradiška (New Town) incorporated the most fashionable Viennese town planning and architectural designs of the epoch. This can be best seen today in the town's main thoroughfare, which is bursting with magnificent Baroque façades.

AQUAE BALISSAE

The Romans were particularly fond of the hot mineral waters that spring naturally from the hills west of Zagreb. They called them Aquae Balissae, and today the two main towns in the area – Lipik and Daruvar – are still renowned spas. Lipik was badly damaged during the recent conflict, so its spa facilities are brand-new (*see pp148–9*).
Lipik: 50km (30 miles) northeast of Nova Gradiška. Tourist information: Marije Terezije 27. Tel: (034) 314 800. Daravur: Tourist office, Julijev Park 1. Tel: (043) 335 499.

Novi Mikanovci

The 13th-century Sveti Bartol (St Bartholomew's) Church in this small village is one of very few predating Ottoman rule that have been left untouched by Islam (most were used as mosques before reverting back to Christian worship after the Ottoman withdrawal). It is known as the Slavonian 'Tower of Pisa' because of its leaning bell tower.

20km (12½ miles) west of Đakovo.
No tourist information.

Osijek

Capital of Slavonia, Osijek is the largest settlement in the east. Always a strategic border post, a self-contained fortified area called Tvrđa forms one distinct element of the town. Gornji Grad (Upper Town) and Donji Grad (Lower Town) make up the whole. The city was inaugurated in 1786 when these – until then disparate – districts were merged. It thrived as a free royal town from 1809, but its position close to the new country border was its undoing during the recent war, when it was consistently bombed by Yugoslav forces. Since being returned to Croatian soil in 1998, it is in the process of a renovation that renders sections of the centre a building site.

Tvrđa was erected at the very start of the 18th century on the banks of the River Drava. Little remains of the curtain walls – only a section and tower in the north – but the interior offers the most complete Baroque ensemble in the region. The cordon of streets is lined with elegant façades, though they lack the grand ornamentation of 'high' Baroque, as it wasn't deemed suitable for a military outpost. Though it did not suffer much damage during the recent fighting, lack of funds for the region means Tvrđa looks a little careworn.

At the heart of Tvrđa is Trg Svetog Trojstva (Holy Trinity Square) with the porticoed Building of the Guard to the west and the long façade of the University, the former regional legislature building, to the north. On the eastern façade the Museum of Slavonia displays artefacts from around the region, including an interesting selection of ancient objects from Roman Mursa, a city that lay on the site of the modern town. The more recent traditional costumes featuring the gold thread that is distinctive to the region add a splash of colour to other galleries. The Jesuit Sv Mihovil (Church of St

Michael), with its distinctive twin-onion-domed façade, is the most important of the religious buildings on the site.

A little way west of Tvrđa is the heart of modern Osijek, with some fine late 19th-century architecture: grand mansions set on tree-lined avenues and squares with cafés and shops. The neo-Gothic Sv Petra i Pavla (Church of Sts Peter and Paul) (known locally as the Cathedral) has an imposing 90m (295ft) tower, but still awaits full renovation to bring its stained-glass windows back to life.

A fine 19th-century mansion plays host to the town's Galerija likovnih umjetnost (Gallery of Fine Arts), with collections of 18th- and 19th-century artists and contemporary canvases. *280km (175 miles) northeast of Zagreb. Tourist Information: Županijska 2. Tel: (031) 203 755; www.tzosijek.hr. Galerija likovnih umjetnost (Gallery of Fine Arts), Europska 9. Tel: (031) 251 280. Open: Tue–Fri 10am–6pm, Sat & Sun 10am–1pm. Admission fee. Museum of Slavonia, Trg Svetog Trojstva 6. Tel: (031) 208 501. Open: Tue–Sat 10am–1pm. Admission fee. Sv Mihovil (Church of St Michael). Tel: (031) 208 990. Open: daily 3–7pm. Sv Petra i Pavla (Church of Sts Peter and Paul). Tel: (031) 310 020. Open: daily 7am–noon & 3–8pm.*

Požega

A centre of Bogomil worship (*see p124*) in the 11th century, the town was ceded to the Knights Templar by King Bela in the 12th century, following which the Franciscans founded a monastery and built the 14th-century Sv Lovre (St Lawrence's) Church.

This Christian tradition came to an abrupt end with the arrival of the Ottomans, but the town rose like a phoenix from the ashes in the wake of the Turkish withdrawal, and there followed a flurry of building including Trg Sv Trojstva (Holy Trinity Square) with its Baroque edifices. The Franjevački Samostan (Franciscan Monastery) was renovated in the early 1700s and a new religious school added. Sv Terezija (St Theresa's) Church was erected in 1763 and is renowned for its murals and frescoes.

60km (37 miles) northeast of Slavonski Brod. Tourist information: Trg Sv Trojstva 1. Tel: (034) 274 900; www.pozega-tz.hr. Franjevački Samostan (Franciscan Monastery) and Sv Lovre (Church of St Lawrence). Trg Sv Trojstva. Tel: (034) 274 553. Open: daily 8am–12.30pm & 5–7pm. Sv Terezija (St Theresa's). Trg Sv Terezija. Tel: (034) 274 321. Open: daily 9am–noon & 3–6pm.

View of Požega

Sisak

Set at the confluence of the Kupa, Ondra and Sava rivers, Sisak has been coveted throughout the centuries for its strategic position. The fortress of Sisak dates from the 1550s and inflicted a massive defeat on the Turks in 1593 that saved the rest of Croatia. In the grounds, the Municipal Museum, housed in an old farmhouse, has many artefacts from the Roman fort of Siscia that once stood on the site.

67km (42 miles) southeast of Zagreb. Tourist information: Rimska ulica. Tel: (044) 522 655.

Slavonski Brod

Set on the Drava River where it overlooks Bosnia-Herzegovina, this town was fortified by the Habsburgs as the border between Viennese and Ottoman territory in the mid-18th century. At that time a fort and 'new town' were built by the Austrians. Today the fort still stands within its curtain walls, but it is rather overgrown.

Outside the walls, the Franciscan Monastery, founded in 1725, is worth a visit for its simple Baroque cloisters and Sv Trojstva (Holy Trinity Church), renovated in the late 20th century. *87km (54 miles) southwest of Osijek. Tourist information: Trg Pobjede 28. Tel: (035) 447 721; www.tzgsb.hr. Franciscan Monastery and Sv Trojstva (Holy Trinity) Church. Tel: (035) 444 533. Open: daily 8am–8pm.*

Vinkovci

An important settlement during the Roman era, Aurelia Cibalae, as it was then known, gave the world the emperor brothers Valens (*c* AD 328–78)

BOGOMIL SECT

The Bogomils were a Medieval Christian sect that believed that God, father of the universe, had two sons – one good (Jesus) and one evil (Satanel). They held that when God created the universe it existed only in the spiritual form, but when Satanel was cast out of heaven he created an alternative universe of physical matter (including humanity). Satanel could not breath life into his creation. He asked God to infuse humanity with a spirit, suggesting they share responsibility for them. God agreed. This meant – so the Bogomils believed – that the earth as matter was intrinsically evil and man was a mixture of good and evil who must strive personally to rid himself of evil. Bogomils rejected the life and death of Jesus, an aspect of scripture that was central to Catholic and Orthodox worship, since they believed he was ethereal matter, This brought them into conflict with the Church authorities. In 1118 the sect leader was burned as a heretic and the group denounced and disbanded.

Franciscan cloisters at Slavonski Brod

and Valentinian (*c* AD 321–75). The town became an early Christian see and the 12th-century Sv Ilija (St Elijah) Church is one of the oldest extant buildings in eastern Croatia. The town's Gradski muzej (Municipal Museum), originally the Habsburg barracks, displays some of the Roman artefacts found in the town.

45km (28 miles) south of Osijek. Tourist information: Trg bana Šokčevica 3.
Tel: (032) 334 653; www.tz-vinkovci.hr.
Gradski muzej (Municipal Museum), Trg bana Šokčevica. Tel: (032) 332 884.
Open: Tue–Fri 10am–1pm & 5–7pm, Sat & Sun 10am–1pm. Admission fee.

Vrpolje

Birthplace of renowned sculptor Ivan Meštrović (1883–1962), the small settlement of Vrpolje has many works donated by the man himself, mostly on display in the Spooman galerija (Spooman Gallery) but including a statue of St John the Baptist in the parish church (Sv Ivan Krstitelj).

40km (25 miles) south of Osijek. No tourist information.

Vukovar

One of the most evocative symbols of the Yugoslav conflict, Vukovar was the scene of both massive bombardment, and some of the worst atrocities of the 1990s. Today the once-fine Baroque town centre is struggling to recover, and much still needs to be done to help the community do the same. UNESCO has stepped in to aid the architectural

The banks of the Danube at Vukovar

rebirth. Perhaps the main purpose of a detour to the town is to gain some understanding of the reality of the recent conflict and to recognise the huge strides that have already been made in other parts of the country.

Typical of the problem is the bullet-riddled fabric of the Gradski muzej (Municipal Museum). This once-majestic Baroque palace displays finds from the region, including some interesting Roman pieces from ancient Vučedol, which lies just south of the modern town.

30km (19 miles) south of Osijek. Tourist information: Strossmayerova 15. Tel: (032) 442 889.

Walk: Osijek

Take a stroll through the history of Austro-Hungarian Croatia, from the Baroque fortified town of Tvrđa that marked the empire's border, to the late 19th-century 'modern town' of neo-Gothic architecture, Gornji Grad. Osijek is still trying to erase the scars of the 20th-century conflict, so you may find sections of the town under scaffolding and some interruptions to this route.

Allow: 3 hours (with museum visits).

Start by exploring Tvrđa, the old fortified town. Built by the Austrians in the wake of the Ottoman withdrawal from this part of the region in 1687, Tvrđa seems more like a village than a defensive structure.

1 Tvrđa

Trg Svetog Trojstva is the heart of the complex, centred on a plague column erected in 1729 by a grateful population who had survived a devastating outbreak. On the western flank is the Building of the Guard, with its incongruously tiny domed clock tower, while in the north is the elegant façade of the University Rector's building, once the administrative headquarters of Slavonia. *On the east flank of the square is the Museum of Slavonia.*

2 The Museum of Slavonia

A leading museum of the region, the Museum of Slavonia combines archaeological and ethnographic collections for an overview of ancient history and traditional lifestyle and costumes of the region. The museum reveals a rich and diverse cultural area whose traditions still survive in numerous local festivals.
Walk north from the square to Trg Vatroslava. On the east flank you'll see the Church of the Holy Cross.

3 Church of the Holy Cross

The church of the Franciscan Monastery was completed in 1720, but houses a revered statue of the Virgin dating from 300 years earlier.
Turn left from the portal of the church, left again at Bosendorfera and left for a third time at Frankulteska.

4 Drava riverside fortifications

From here you can walk through the only remaining gate of Tvrđa for views of the surviving riverside fortifications.
Return to Trg Svetog Trojstva and leave by Franje Kuhaca on its southern side. Turn right at the next junction to Trg Križanića to find the Church of St Michael.

The Church of the Holy Cross

children's playground and a range of statuary. Europska Avenija links the fort with Gornji Grad.

6 Europska Avenija

Europska boasts some fine 19th-century mansions set in ample gardens. Number 9 houses the Gallery of Fine Arts, with a collection of canvases, mainly by Croatian artists, encompassing the 18th, 19th and 20th centuries, including a number by artists of the little-known Osijek School.

Continue down Europska. It becomes Kapucinska as you enter Gornji Grad. This leads to Trg A Starčevića, where you'll find the Church of Sts Peter and Paul.

5 Church of St Michael

The twin domes of this early 18th-century church stand tall over the rooftops of the fort. The portal of the Jesuit monastery to which it belongs is also worth admiring.

Leave Tvrđa along Franje Kuhača (passing the walls of the Jesuit Monastery and the Church of St Michael on the right). This is a grand avenue flanked by formal and informal parkland – there's a

7 Church of Sts Peter and Paul

With its imposing tower, this neo-Gothic church dominates downtown Osijek. The stained-glass windows that were the pride of the church were damaged during the war and are only slowly being renovated.

You can take refreshment in one of the cafés of Trg A Starčevića amongst its late 19th-century façades.

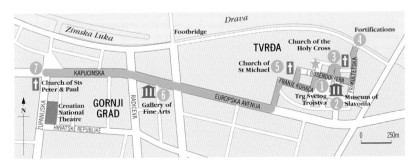

Northern Croatia

The green, rolling hills of Croatia's most northerly lands – bounded by Slovenia and Hungary at the western flank of the Panonnian Plain – are collectively known as the Zagorje. Controlled by the Habsburg Empire for many centuries, it has excellent castles and forts as well as numerous Baroque treasures to enjoy, from palaces to churches. It is also full of natural wonders, including mineral spas and acres of vineyards, lying off the main tourist routes. Many attractions mentioned here can easily be reached in a day trip from Zagreb.

Belec

The village of Belec exemplifies the development in religious architecture in Croatia, with its two major churches. On the outer fringes of the town the older St George's Church is one of very few Romanesque buildings to have survived in this region. The simple exterior is dominated by its bell tower, while the interior displays original frescoes. In total contrast, below the village, is Sveta Marija Snježna (St Mary of the Snows), a Baroque *tour de force* built in 1674. It has an exceptionally ornate interior. The typical fluid lines are further enhanced by *trompe-l'oeil* frescoes by the master painter Ivan Ranger (*see p130*).

If the churches are closed, contact the tourist information office in Marija Bistrica (*see p130*) for an appointment to view.

25km (15½ miles) north of Marija Bistrica. No tourist information.

Čakovec

Čakovec is inextricably linked with the history of Croatia, the ducal family and their castle being at the centre of many major historical developments over the centuries. Count Chaky built the first defensive tower, Chaktornya, in the late 13th century. This was developed over the following 100 years to include a diminutive but sturdy castle. In 1547 the domain was gifted by Emperor Ferdinand to Nikola Zrinski, then governor of Croatia, for his help in defeating the Ottomans. Zrinski's family later developed the castle, adding curtain walls and a more luxurious 'palace', but they eventually lost the castle after the attempt to wrest Croatia from Hungary went badly awry.

Under the control of the Austro-Hungarian empire, a grand Baroque palace was built beside the old castle. The two offer a contrasting view of noble daily life throughout the centuries, though they are rather careworn and certain elements are undergoing long-term renovations. *9km (5½ miles) north of Varaždin. Tourist information: Kralja Tomislava 2. Tel: (040) 313 319; www.tourism-cakovec.hr*

Krapina

Well known in palaeontology circles, in 1899 this small town saw the discovery of *Homo krapinensis* (Krapina Man), a

Shrine to Marshal Tito in Kumrovec

Neanderthal specimen. Many of Krapina Man's artefacts are on view in the tiny Museum of Evolution. *45km (28 miles) north of Zagreb. Tourist information: Magistratska 11. Tel: (049) 371 330. Museum of Evolution, Šetalište v. Slug bb. Tel: (049) 371 491; www.krapina.com. Open: daily 9am–5pm. Admission fee.*

Kumrovec

This tiny village close to the Slovenian border is the birthplace of Josip Broz (Marshal Tito), founder and father of communist Yugoslavia. During his rule, much of the village was preserved. It now functions as an ethnological complex. Muzej Staro Selo (Old Village Museum) also re-creates late

19th-century life in this part of the world. Eighteen buildings have been preserved, with workshops of crafts such as weaving, wine-making and blacksmithing, and from June to September you'll find artisans working here. You can visit Tito's humble birthplace, a traditional cottage, which displays the family's furniture and other belongings.

48km (30 miles) northwest of Zagreb.
Tourist information: Cesta Lijepe naše 6a. Tel: (049) 502 044.
Muzej Staro Selo (Old Village Museum), 49295 Kumrovec. Tel: (049) 225 830; www.mdc.hr/kumrovec. Open: daily Apr–Sept 9am–7pm & Oct–Mar 9am–4pm. Admission fee.

Lepoglava

Lepoglava's 15th-century Pauline monastery, originally a great centre of learning, was turned into a prison after the dissolution of the order in the 1850s. It became notorious throughout Croatia for its harsh regime (Tito was imprisoned here for his anti-Fascist views, then Tuđman for his pro-Croat sentiments). Today, the prison functions separately, and the monastery is slowly being renovated. The Baroque Sv Marija (Blessed Virgin Mary) Church is the highlight of the complex. Inside is the largest single collection of works by the great Baroque artist Ivan Ranger. Born in the Tyrol in 1700, Ranger joined the Pauline movement and reached his peak as an artist whilst living in the Lepoglava community.

Lepoglava was also famed for its lace, and still has a lace-making school, but there is none for sale in the town.
27km (17 miles) southwest of Varaždin.
Tourist information: Trg 1 hrvatskog sveučilišta 3. Tel: (042) 791 090.

Ludbreg

During a Mass in 1411, a priest at Ludbreg Franciscan monastery claimed he saw the wine in the sacramental cup turn to blood. A pilgrimage site grew up here which was given the papal seal of approval in 1513. Today the miraculous chalice is housed in its own sanctuary – the Chapel of the Special Blood of Christ – in Sv Trojstvo (the Holy Trinity Sanctuary), which was built in the 16th century but much altered in the 18th and 19th centuries.
20km (12½ miles) east of Varaždin.
Tourist information: Trg Sveta Trojstva 14. Tel: (042) 810 690; www.tz-ludbreg.hr

Marija Bistrica

This village plays host to Sv Marija Snježna (St Mary of the Snows) which, like Ludbreg (*see above*), is one of the most revered pilgrimage sites in Croatia. Its miraculous statue of the *Black Madonna with Child* was found totally unblemished after fierce Ottoman bombardment of the church and village. The present sanctuary dates from 1883 and, in addition to the statue, contains some fine religious treasures donated by pilgrims. On the way to the portal, visitors climb through replicas of the Stations of the Cross in Jerusalem.

25km (15½ miles) north of Zagreb. Tourist information: Zagrebacka. Tel: (049) 468 380; www.marija-bistrica.hr

Sv Marija Snježna (St Mary of the Snows), Trg pape Ivana Pavla II. Tel: (049) 468 360. Open: daily 8am–6pm. Free.

Trakošćan

The castle at Trakošćan, originally founded in the 13th century, stood at the forefront of action against the Ottoman Turks, protecting the southern boundary of the Habsburg Empire. Following the easing of the threat in the 17th century, it became the property of the Drašković counts, and was transformed in the 19th century into the sumptuous neo-Gothic family palace we see today. The castle museum displays family furniture, portraits and other family heirlooms, and you can enjoy the English-style gardens complete with lake and parkland.

Trakošćan Castle, 42254 Trakošćan. Tel: (042) 796 281; www.mdc.hr/trakoscan. Open: May–Sept daily 9am–3pm, Oct–Apr daily 9am–6pm. Admission fee.

Varaždin

Croatia's 'Little Vienna', Varaždin, is the most complete Baroque town in the country, rebuilt after fire consumed the medieval settlement in 1776. Set on the south bank of Croatia's natural northern border, the Drava River, and declared a free town in 1209, it held a position of strategic importance throughout the second millennium. In recent years it has grown to become the largest town in the north.

Northern Croatia

The Pauline monastery at Lepoglava was once a notorious prison

Stari Grad (Old Town) is a late 13th-century to late 18th-century castle complex, with disparate towers linked by 16th-century Renaissance wings. Today it houses the Gradski muzej (Varaždin Municipal Museum), with its collections of furniture and traditional handicrafts.

In the heart of town, the Gradska Vijećnica (Town Hall) has been in continuous use since 1523. The building itself is original, but the interior has been redeveloped in the intervening centuries. During the summer you'll find the uniformed Purgari guard in attendance, as they have been since 1750, complete with their bearskin hats. Trg kralja Tomislava (Tomislav Square) is home to several other fine buildings, including the 17th-century Dvor Drašković (Drašković Palace), and there are other excellent façades in the surrounding streets.

Two churches are worth particular mention. Uznesenja Marijina (Cathedral of the Assumption) was built in the early 17th century but only upgraded to cathedral status in 1997. The Baroque interior is splendid, the white walls contrasting with the high décor of the altars. Meanwhile, the Franciscan Monastery has ceiling frescoes by master Ivan Ranger, and its church Sv Ivana Krstitelja (St John the Baptist) has a renowned ornate gilded pulpit.

77km (48 miles) north of Zagreb. Tourist information: Ivana Padovca 3. Tel: (042) 210 987; www.tourism-varazdin.hr. Gradski muzej (Varaždin Municipal Museum), Strossmayerovo 7. Tel: (042) 212 918; www.varazdin.hr. Open: Tue–Fri 10am–6pm, Sat & Sun 10am–1pm. Admission fee. Gradska Vijećnica (Town Hall), Trg kralja Tomislava. Tel: (042) 402 506. Changing of the Guard: Saturdays at noon.

Varaždinske Toplice

One of a collection of northern spa towns, Varaždinske Toplice has offered wealthy visitors a place to relax for centuries. It was popular during Roman times, but fell into disuse after the empire crumbled. It was only during the development of the 'modern' resort in the 18th century that the Roman spa was rediscovered under metres of mud (at Ivana Krstitelja Lalenguea Vrt).

The Varaždinske Toplice Zavičajni muzej (Varaždinske Toplice Old Town Museum), housed in the fine 17th-century Baroque castle at the heart of the tiny medieval district, has many Roman artefacts that have been found in the region.

Baroque detail at Varaždin

Modern spa facilities at Varaždinske Toplice

15km (9½ miles) southeast of Varaždin. Tourist office: Trg Slobode 16. Tel: (042) 633 133.
Varaždinske Toplice Zavičajni muzej (Varaždinske Toplice Old Town Museum), Trg Solbode 16. Tel: (042) 633 339. Open: Mon & Wed–Fri 9am–2pm, Tue 9am–5pm, Sat 9am–1pm. Admission fee.

Veliki Tabor

An exceptional medieval hilltop stronghold, Dvor Veliki Tabor, is the only reason to visit the tiny, remote settlement of Desinić, which nestles against the Slovakian border. But for castle lovers it is worth the trip! Erected in the 14th century, it became the domain and family home of the Ratkaj family, and has changed very little in the intervening centuries. The defensive outer walls, with their large round towers and few tiny windows, guard the palace, whilst the interior has three storeys with porticoed corridors overlooking a small courtyard. Renovation work is ongoing.
20km (12½ miles) northeast of Kumrovec. No tourist information.
Dvor Veliki Tabor, Desnić. Tel: (049) 434 963. Open: daily 10am–5pm. Admission fee.

Vinica

The first arboretum on Croatian soil was founded here in the late 19th century. Opeka Park is now a nature reserve, replete with exotic species from around the world, many collected by the park's original creator, Count Bombelles.
20km (12½ miles) west of Varaždin. Tourist information: Vinica 5. Tel: (042) 722 233.
Opeka Park. Open daylight hours. Free.

The castle complex of Veliki Tabor

Walk: Varaždin

Croatia's Baroque masterpiece, Varaždin, presents a riot of colour – from pastel façades to bright window boxes in full bloom. It is the whole of the downtown heart of the town (rather than the individual parts) that makes Varaždin special. This is a living town, where shops and cafés inhabit historic buildings: you are even sightseeing when you are relaxing!

Allow: 3 hours (including attraction visits).

Start at the tourist office, itself installed in a renovated old building. Turn right out of the door and make the short walk to Trg M Stančića.

1 Sermage Palace

Named after a Croatian writer, this square is home to Sermage Dvor (Sermage Palace), now the Galerija Starih i Novi Majstora (Gallery of Old and New Masters), which has works by lesser lights of the Flanders/Dutch movement such as Adrian Cornelius and Jan Both, and by pupils of the Canaletto School.

Stari Grad fortress

Walk straight ahead from the palace across the drawbridge of the Watch Tower into the Gardens of Stari Grad.

2 Stari Grad

This parkland was, until the last century, the castle moat, created during the Renaissance redevelopment of the complex. Explore the castle and museum located within.

Leave Stari Grad via Uršulinska, passing the Ursuline Church and Nunnery on your right. Turn left at the second intersection onto Franjevački Trg and continue until you see a bronze statue on your left.

3 Grgur Ninski statue

This is Grgur Ninski (early Christian Bishop of Nin on the Dalmatian Coast near Zadar), created in bronze by Ivan Meštrović (*see p23*). It was originally due to be erected in Split but when completed it was deemed too small.

Split got a larger version (*see p94*) and Varaždin gained this original. Rub his big toe as you make a wish – it's bound to come true.

Behind the statue you'll see the façade of the Franciscan Church of John the Baptist, with ceiling frescoes by Ivan Ranger.

Continue to walk along Franjevački Trg, past the fine façade of Patačić Palace (1764) on your right. This was the centre of society life in the town in the 18th century. Continue into Trg Tomislava.

Trg Tomislava is in the heart of Varaždin

4 Trg Tomislava

Across the square to your left you'll see the Town Hall, home of the city administration since 1523. Directly ahead is the palace of the Drašković family, which was rebuilt in 1756, and became the seat of the short-lived Croatian Parliament and Regency Council in the late 1700s. Immediately to your left are the arches of Ritz House, built during the Renaissance in around 1540. There has been a coffee house here for more than a century. Look on the façades for old shop signs – a stylised mermaid where fish was once sold, or the Iron Man denoting the ironmonger's.

Leave the square via Pavlinska (directly opposite the way you entered the square). Fifty metres (160ft) along on the right you'll see the modern, heavy bronze doors of the Cathedral.

5 Cathedral of the Ascension

This is one of the finest Baroque religious interiors in Croatia.

Return to Trg Tomislava and walk towards Franjevački Trg, but take a left at Gundulića, known to everyone as 'Shop Street'. At the end of Gundulića is Trg Slobode, or Freedom Square, where you'll find the Parish Church of St Nicholas.

6 Church of St Nicholas

Legend has it that this church (1761) was built on top of a bear den, and that its first visitor was a female bear back from the nearby forests, searching for her cubs. When she couldn't find them she was so grief-stricken that she turned to stone. Her statue has been incorporated into the church tower.

Return to Trg Tomislava to enjoy refreshment in the square.

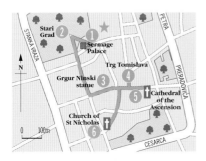

Croatian wine

When Miljenco (Mike) Grgich announced in the late 1990s that he was investing in a large project in his native Croatia, the wine world certainly took notice. Grgich had been one of the major players in Californian wine since the 1970s. Croatia is 'small potatoes' as a wine exporter, but visit any supermarket while you are there and you'll find a bewildering range of domestic labels. These bear witness to the existence of a substantial wine industry – fertile ground for Grgich.

Currently the country has 57,094ha (141,079 acres) of land under vine. Inland, 90 per cent of production is white, while the coast and islands produce mainly reds. Each island has its unique soil type and temperature variations, so acidity, colour and tannin content can vary, even between wines from adjoining islands or domains. Most producers still work on a small scale, and local cooperatives play an important role in the industry (*see pp116–17*).

Grape varieties

Croatia has a large number of domestic grape varieties, many with ancient antecedents. The most common grape in the hinterland is the gravesina, while on the coast it is malvasia. Others include franken, debit, posip, zlahtina, marastina, vugava, grk and plavac. Since the 1970s, major international grape varieties have been increasing in popularity and you'll see many generic bottles of Riesling, Gewürztraminer, Chardonnay, Merlot and Cabernet Sauvignon.

Standards

Much Croatian wine production is in the '*vin de table*' style. Small farmers and many restaurants and households make their own perfectly palatable – if young and fruity – tipples that sit perfectly with the grilled meats, fish and salads that we eat when on holiday. However, Croatia has introduced the Protected Geographical Origin status for wine

Grapes ripening on the vine

A selection of Croatian wines

(similar to the AOC standard in France). This now accounts for just less than half of the total, said to come to 50 million bottles.

Useful wine phrases

dry *suho*
dessert *desertno*
geographical origin *geografsko porijeklo*
quality *kvalitetno*
red *crveno*
sparkling *pjenusavo*
sweet *slatko*
white *bijelo*
wine *vino*

Where and what to buy

We can only scratch the surface here, and in any case one of the pleasures of drinking wine is the exploration of new labels and the savouring of a new vintage. For the better-quality labels, prices in Croatia are not cheap. Croatians themselves are beginning to recognise that some vineyards produce excellent products that merit a higher price.

LYNN ALLEY, WINE SPECTATOR, WEDNESDAY 23 JANUARY 2003

'The hidden origins of California's Zinfandel grape have at last been uncovered, according to a prominent grapevine geneticist Carole Meredith, who is known for her discoveries of the parent of Cabernet Sauvignon, Chardonnay and Syrah. Using DNA-profiling techniques, Meredith and two Croatian scientists, Ivan Pejić and Edi Maletić, discovered in December that Zinfandel and an indigenous Croatian grape called Crljenačk are one and the same.'
For more information on this story visit www.crozinfandel.com

The Dingač grape, bottled as a generic wine and produced in the Potomlje region on Pelješac, is probably the country's best-regarded wine. It is full-bodied and fruity and can be laid down to age. Postup is similar to Dingač but drier. Wines produced in the Donja banda are also admired. In Istria the Teran reds have an intense, almost black colour, while Momjan is a honey-coloured sweet wine. The islands generally most noted for wine are Brač, Korčula and Pag.

Testing the product

Getting away from it all

Countless intimate rocky coves, uninhabited islands, mountain peaks, rivers and managed nature reserves means it's not difficult to get away from your fellow tourists, even when – as in Dubrovnik or Rovinj – the whole world seems to be sightseeing. Croatia has some exceptional national parks and protected landscapes safeguarding several pristine environments.

If you love nature, especially bird-watching (see *pp98–9*), then it is worth leaving your sun bed and putting your tan on hold for a day or two in order to go and enjoy arguably the finest wetland habitats in Europe. A boat trip is the perfect retreat, especially if you don't have to share it with other paying passengers (*see information on sailing in Croatia, pp168–9*). Alternatively, you can get your hiking boots on and head for the mountains and the fantastic views just inland from the Dalmatian and Istrian coasts.

NATIONAL PARKS
Brijuni National Park

This small group of islands just off the Istrian coast protects excellent tracts of unspoilt Mediterranean vegetation. In the 19th century they became the private domain of an Austrian industrialist, and during the communist era they became the playground of President Tito, and were only open to his invited guests.

Today the two main islands – Veli Brijun (Greater Brijun) and Mali Brijun (Lesser Brijun) – are open to visitors. The larger island has a safari park, a small collection of exotic animals that were offered as diplomatic gifts to Tito when he was in power. These include his old parrot, which apparently knows quite a few Croatian swearwords! There are also some fine Roman and Byzantine remains, as well as a golf course that lies close to Brijun village.

Brijuni National Park information, Brijunska 10, Fažana. Tel: (052) 525 888; www.brijuni.hr. Open: at all hours, but access is by boat at set times from the mainland. Fažana and Pula are the closest ports. Be aware that not all boat trips actually stop at the islands: some offer a two-hour cruise around the Brijuni chain instead. Admission fee. Tickets for tours of the island are available from the Brijuni National Park office at the harbour in Fažana.

Kornati Islands National Park

Croatians have a legend that when God had finished creating the world he found he had a small collection of white rocks left. He casually tossed them into the water off the coast of Dalmatia, and when he looked again he found he had created perfection in the form of the Kornati Islands.

The largest archipelago of islands off the Croatian – or, to be more precise, the Dalmatian – coast, in fact the largest in the Adriatic, the Kornati group consists of almost 150 separate tracts of land scattered over 230sq km (89sq miles) of sea. The Kornati Islands National Park was established in 1980. It protects reefs and waters as well as the islands: in fact 75 per cent of the protected area is water.

There are no rivers or streams on the Kornati; it is pure karst substrate that is cut by fissures and indented by caves and grottoes. The white limestone lying under the coastal shallows is what gives the waters their heavenly blue colour. The cliffs in the southwest, which are up to 80m (262ft) in height, are the highest coastal features along the Croatian Adriatic.

Kornat is easily the largest island, and gives its name to the whole group. It is 25km (16 miles) in length, but very narrow, and measures just over 32sq km (12sq miles) in total. The islands were last inhabited in the 18th century, though Illyrian settlements have been excavated, and the Romans carved a large water cistern here in the first century AD to supply their fleet. Though there are small seasonal settlements, the Kornatis are a sailor's paradise, replete with innumerable quiet coves. The only marina is at Piskara. It has 120 berths.

Kornati Islands National Park information, Butina 2, Murter. Tel: (022) 435 740; www.kornati.hr. Admission fee.

There are almost 150 islands in the Kornati archipelago

Krka National Park

The Krka River runs through deep limestone canyons and into a string of lakes formed by natural dams and waterfalls before flowing out into the Adriatic near Šibenik (northern Dalmatia). Unlike the Plitvice Lakes (*see p143*), the Krka watercourses are easily visited by organised boat tours, the longest taking four hours.

Two of the most visited spots are waterfalls. Skradinski Buk is a magnificent, 50m (164ft) high waterfall that cascades over huge boulders covered in mosses and other water-loving plants; Roški Slap is wider and shorter than its sibling but creates a maze of white-water chutes. A tiny idyllic offshore islet in Lake Visovac plays host to a Franciscan Monastery founded in the mid-15th century.

Tickets for entrance and boat tours are available at Skradin park entrance (from where you can take a boat into the park), or from Lozovac and Roški Slap road entrances.

Krka Park information, Trg Ivana Pavla 5, Šibenik. Tel: (022) 201 777; www.npkrka.hr. Admission fee.

Mljet National Park

Only the westernmost section of this long thin island offshore from Dubrovnik is classified as a national park. It protects rare and unbroken tracts of verdant Aleppo pine forests, plus their surrounding coastal shallows. The island was once part of the Republic of Ragusa (*see pp112–3*) and boasts some fine 16th- and 17th-century buildings. The coastline is characterised by deep sinkholes and inlets, which now form sheltered coves for yachtsmen and provide excellent places for snorkelling. The old St Mary's Monastery, founded in the 12th century, was used as a hotel until 1991, but is today undergoing a process of renovation.

The east of the island has several fishing villages that still eschew tourism. Saplunara beach, in the southeast and out of the national park area, is one of the finest in Dalmatia. *Mljet National Park information, Pristanište 2, Doveđari. Tel: (020) 744 041; www.np-mljet.hr. Admission fee.*

Paklenica National Park

This park protects the canyons of the Mala and Velika Paklenica gorges, up to 400m (1,312ft) deep, which cut deep into the Velebit mountain range. The largest massif in Croatia, this is a karst limestone region with a wealth of fine caves (more than 70, though only one, the Manita Cave, is open to the public).

The rugged coastline of limestone and pine

The stark beauty of Paklenica National Park in Dalmatia

The region also produces excellent mineral water. Despite its austere appearance – sheer white cliffs of stone – the Paklenica is a rich living environment. The park protects an important black pine forest with unusual dwarf species, but also rare areas of bellflower and a unique species of sandwort (*Arenaria orbicularis*). Animals include the brown bear, lynx, wolf and several species of deer. Over 200 species of bird can be seen in the park throughout the year, though only 97 species nest here. Eighty-two species of butterfly have been documented, along with more than 31 species of amphibian and 12 types of snakes.

Within the park you'll find an underground bunker built by the Yugoslav Army as a shelter. The 1,730sq m (18,621sq ft) of tunnels, a veritable underground city, is now used as an exhibition space but they are currently closed for renovations. In the north a tropical garden brings more profuse life to the slopes, whilst you'll also find the remains of seven early 19th-century watermills scattered around the park; these were still being used in the 1960s. Manita Peć (Manita Cave) is 175m (574ft) in length and must be visited with a park guide (*arrangements with the park office, see details below*).

Within the Paklenica you'll also find Sjeverni Velebit National Park, covering the northern Velebit region around the Velebit Peak itself. This tiny park protects what is regarded as the most beautiful wild and rugged tracts of mountainscape.

Paklenica National Park information, 23244 Starigrad-Paklenika. Tel: (023)

369 155; www.paklenica.hr.
Admission fee.
Sjeverni Velebit National Park. Tel: (053)
665 380; www.np-sjeverni-velebit.hr.
Admission fee.

Plitvice Lakes National Park

First protected in 1949, Plitvice Lakes
became a World Heritage Site in 1979.
At just under 30,000ha (74,130 acres),
the park covers the headwaters of the
Korana River, a karst (limestone) river
basin that has been eroded to create an
exceptional landscape of 16 pristine
azure lakes linked by cascades and
waterfalls and surrounded by verdant
forest. The area can be explored by
a series of well laid-out wooden
boardwalks and footpaths, with ferry
routes across the lakes, while motorised
(truck-drawn carriages) train services
allow you to shorten the full 16km
(10-mile) circuit.

Waterfalls at Plitvice

Within the park boundaries you'll
find the *ćorkova uvala* virgin forest,
which has rare specimens of coniferous
species reaching up to 50m (164ft) in
height. Fauna includes European brown
bears, wolf, eagle owl and capercaillie.
There are two park entrances with
information offices. Access to the park is
via a series of preset, well laid-out paths.
For information: Plitvice Lakes Public
Establishment, 53231 Plitvice Lakes.
Tel: (053) 751 015; www.np-plitvicka-
jezera.hr. Admission fee.

Risnjak National Park

One of Croatia's smaller national parks,
Risnjak – set around Risnjak peak
(1,528m/5,013ft) – protects the karst
highlands of Gorski Kotar in northwestern Croatia, just north of Rijeka.
It is a pristine landscape with neither
human habitation nor cultivation.

The most forested part of the
country, the Risnjak, is where most
snow falls. It also forms the watershed
between the Adriatic and Black Sea
river drainage basins. Every stream
on its western slopes flows into the
Adriatic; water draining from its
eastern slopes begins the long journey
through six other countries to the
mouth of the Danube.

This park has swathes of coniferous
and broad-leaved forest, with beech,
fir, spruce, sycamore and elm being
the predominant species. At higher
altitudes trees become stunted and
bent due to heavy snowfall. Alpine
meadows are ideal environments for

One of the 16 lakes that make Plitvice Lakes National Park so beautiful

flowers such as edelweiss, mountain orchids and alpine rock rose. Animals include the wild cat, the lynx, brown bear, chamois and abundant deer. *Risnjak National Park information, Bijela vodica 48, Crni Lug. Tel: (051) 836 133; www.risnjak.hr – but information is not in English. Admission fee.*

NATURE PARKS

Nature parks have a category of protection that is less stringent than that of the national parks and often brings human settlement and land cultivation into the equation. Activity is allowed provided it doesn't endanger the *raison d'être* of the park.

Biokovo

Above Makarska River. Exceptionally picturesque limestone peaks with some of the best landscapes in Croatia. *For information, tel: (021) 616 924; www.biokovo.com*

Kopački Rit

East of Osijek. One of the largest marshland environments in Europe, Kopački Rit is situated at the intersection of the Drava and Danube rivers. It is home to a wide range of flora and fauna, including white willow, a large deer population, and herons, lapwings, terns, cormorants and many migratory birds. *For information, tel: (031) 750 855; www.kopacki-rit.com*

Lonjsko polje

East of Sisak. Set on the floodplain of the Drava River, Lonjsko polje is a large seasonal swampland of exceptional oak forest and abundant bird life, including rare black storks. A landscape managed by humans, it offers abundant summer pasture for horses and cattle. *For information, tel: (044) 672 080; www.pp-lonjsko-polje.hr*

Medvednica

The playground for the capital, this mountain is a great place for hiking and picnics and is known for its caves and verdant valleys. A skier's paradise in winter, it is home hill for the successful Kostelic family.
For information, tel: (01) 4586 317;
www.pp-medvednica.hr

Papuk

In Slavonia. A volcanic mountain peak.
For information, tel: (034) 313 030;
www.pp-papuk.hr

Telašćica

Close to the Kornati National Park. A narrow fissure cut into the tallest cliffs on the island of Dugi Otok.
For information, tel: (023) 377 096;
www.telascica.hr

Učka

Istrian mountains offering magnificent views of Kvarner Bay.
For information, tel: (051) 293 753;
www.pp-ucka.hr

Zumberak Samoborsko Gorge

Popular with residents of the capital for its pretty villages and meadowland.
For information, tel: (01) 332 7660;
www.pp-zumberak-samoborsko-gorje.hr

STRICT RESERVES

A strict reserve is applied when the geomorphic structure of the earth is the focus of attention. Two of these reserves exist in Croatia.

Bijele I Samarske Stijene

This reserve protects a section of the central Velika Kapela mountain range with its unique limestone rock layers, folded into surreal shapes by the immense pressure of the earth's tectonic plates.

Hajdučki Rožanski Kukova

The very highest peaks of the Velebit are protected here, with their spectacular limestone bluffs and huge caves.

MISCELLANEOUS PARKS AND RESERVES
Limski Canal (*see pp51–2*)

Palud Ornithological Reserve

Eight kilometres (5 miles) south of the Rovinj, this is the only reserve specifically for birds in Istria. It protects over 200 species of birds, including game species such as pheasant and partridge, which are widely hunted elsewhere. Guided

Many national parks can only be visited on foot

Head off on a wooden boat for an island adventure

tours can be arranged through the Rovinj tourist office.

Vransko Jezero (Lake Vransko)

Lying between Zadar and Šibenik on the northern Dalmatian coast, this is the largest lake in Croatia, with vast tracts of reed beds offering breeding grounds and habitat to gulls, herons, egrets and other wading birds. It is protected as the Vransko Jezero Ornitološki Rezervat (Lake Vransko Ornithological Reserve).
Information office, Trg Petra Svačića 2, Biograd. Tel: (023) 383 181; www.vransko-jezero.hr

Zlatni Rt (Golden Cape) Park Forest

On the southern outskirts of Rovinj, this park protects ancient dark evergreen forest – cedars, cypresses and Aleppo pines plus tracts of virgin holm oak – set beside several coastal bays. It's the perfect place for strolling and there are several cafés close to the largest lidos, which are popular places for swimming and sunbathing.

There is an information point at the park where it's possible to rent bikes and head out on a guided tour through the forest – in early or late season contact ProMontana, tel: (052) 384 184 – or around the park's seawall. Guided walks in the Palud swamp can also be arranged.

ISLAND ADVENTURES

The waters around Croatia offer the perfect environment for some R&R, and even from the smallest of resorts you should be able to take boat trips to offshore islands, or along the coast to sheltered coves and beaches.

From **Rovinj** (*see pp57–8*) you can take boat trips into **Lim Bay** (known locally as Limski Canal) (*see pp51–2*), take the ferry trip out to **St Katherine's Island**, or further offshore to cruise around the many smaller islands.

From **Cres** and **Losinj** you can take day tours around – or scheduled ferries to – the smaller offshore islands. These include **Ilovik**, where hundreds of ancient amphorae have been discovered; **Susak**, an island composed solely of sand, and **Unije**, which is blanketed in olive groves.

From **Krk** take in the three smallest islands of the **Krk Archipelago** (with an hour on each) from the harbour. *Mali Gospa* is one of many boats that make this trip. *Tel: (051) 222 295.*

Zadar makes an ideal jumping-off point for the Kornati Islands National Park (*see p139*). ITA tourist agency offer trips daily from Zadar port. *Tel: (023) 373 885; www.ita.hr*

From **Dubrovnik** there are regular water-taxis out to **Lokrum** or boats further afield to one or more of the **Elaphite Islands**, lying north along the shore from the city.

There's good two-way traffic between **Brač** and **Hvar**. Take a boat trip from **Bol** to **Hvar Town** or other parts of the island. The *Veritas* boat leaves from the harbour in Bol. *Tel: (021) 635 239.*

One of the best travel agencies to contact for all types of organised experiences is Atlas Travel (*www.atlas-croatia.com*). They have offices at all the major resorts along the Croatian coast and have an excellent reputation.

Getting away from it all

Coastal waters provide the perfect playground for yachties

Spa treatments

Everyone is entitled to a little pampering, and if you are looking for somewhere different to spend a little 'downtime', try a Croatia spa. Croatia has an exceptional wealth of natural mineral springs that have formed the basis of treatments for centuries. The Romans had a love of bathing – it was almost as much about socialising as cleanliness. Some of the most renowned spas in the Roman Empire were in north and east Croatia, grouped together as the Aquae Ballisae (see p120).

Victorian Europe discovered complementary medicines in the mid-19th century, and doctors would happily prescribe a sojourn in the mountains or on the coast as a treatment for a range of conditions. Grand spas throughout the Austro-Hungarian Empire were filled with clients including writers, composers, playwrights – and even royalty.

Under Communism, the Croats became used to being prescribed complementary therapies as part of an underfunded and non-innovative health service. So much so that they are still regarded as mainstream treatments for skin disorders, high blood pressure, breathing problems, arthritis, nervous conditions, and kidney and liver complaints. In the spas around the country you won't just find the wealthy 'de-stressing', but you'll also find people from all walks of life in search of relief from documented medical conditions.

Energy Clinic (*www.energyclinic.com*) is a new company with modern 'Wellness Centres' offering a range of relaxation, massage, beauty and anti-cellulite treatments. The centres are normally affiliated with a good-standard hotel. You can find them at:
Hotel Westin, I Krsnjvoga 1, Zagreb.
Tel: (01) 485 2900.
Hotel Argentina, Dubrovnik.
Tel: (020) 440 596.
Frankopanska 10, Cavtat.
Tel: (020) 475 555
There is a new clinic at the Hotel Odisej on Mljet.

Hotel Bizovacke Toplice
A spa near Osijek discovered in the 20th century. Medicinal springs rich in minerals, plus electrotherapy and general spa treatments.
Suncana 39, 31222 Bizovac.
Tel: (031) 685 180. Fax: (031) 685 188; www.bizovacke-toplice.hr

An all-over mud wrap treatment

Hotel Korinjak

This hotel runs what it calls 'soul vacations' in the summer: full-board vegetarian packages with yoga, stress reduction, and other therapies.
Veli Iž, Iž Island. Tel: (023) 277 064; www.korinjak.hr

Hotel Sol Umag

Sol umag is a four-star hotel has a 'wellness and beauty' centre and good sporting facilities.
Jadranska bb, 52470 Umag. Tel: (052) 714 000. Fax: (052) 714 999; www.solmelia.com

Terme Selce

On the northern Dalmatian coast, south of Crikvenica. Full diagnostic and therapeutic facilities.
1 prilaz I. L Ribara 8, 51266 Selce. Tel:

THE SPA ALPHABET

Acupuncture – thin needles are inserted into the skin to activate pressure points or nerve-endings

Aromatherapy – use of essential oils to improve mood or ameliorate minor conditions

Detox or detoxification – the process of removing toxins from the body

Exfoliation – removal of the upper layers of the epidermis to eliminate toxins and promote new skin growth

Helio-prophylaxis – sunlight therapy

Inhalations – used to treat lung problems and for reoxygenation of the system

Mud treatments – used to infuse minerals into or leach toxins out of the skin

Ozone and oxygen therapy – like an ozone 'sauna' to eliminate free radicals.

Reflexology – central to this therapy is the belief that areas of the feet are linked to areas of the body and that massage of these points will promote improvement in problem areas

Seaweed wrap – the body is coated in seaweed extract to remineralise and rehydrate the skin

Thalassotherapy – the use of seawater for massage

Toxins – substances that are damaging to or poisonous for the body, such as coffee or alcohol

(051) 764 055. Fax: (051) 768 310; www.terme-selce.hr

Thalassotherapia Crikvenica

Good range of thalassotherapy and other wellbeing treatments.
Gajevo setaliste 21, 51260 Crikvenica. Tel: (051) 407 666. Fax: (051) 785 018.

Shopping

Browsing in the narrow streets of an old Venetian port on a summer evening is one of the delights of shopping in Croatia. The country is reclaiming traditional crafts, but it is happening slowly, and handmade goods are still less easy to find than mass-produced souvenirs. In many major shopping streets you'll find familiar high-street names and brands catering to young and fashionable Croatians.

Embroidery and lace

Embroidery and lace-making have been traditional activities for women for centuries. For the best lace head to the island of Pag, whose women have a particularly high reputation for the quality of their work. For the best embroidery, the intricate patterns in gold and silver thread on items made in Osijek are hard to beat.

Foodstuffs

Food that travels well always makes an excellent souvenir. The wines produced in Croatia may not be internationally known but they will not disappoint; the same is true of preserved jams and honeys, or olive oils. Try mustard if you visit Samobor near Zagreb; dried or preserved truffles are a must from Istria. You can also buy the *paški sir* (sheep's cheese) on Pag. Croatia produces excellent distillates. Slivovic is perhaps the most famous, a strong plum brandy that is excellent after dinner. The grape-based *grappa* or *rakia* is also popular.

Art

There's no shortage of original art on sale in Croatia, where the wonderful landscapes and exquisite architecture make excellent subjects. The most atmospheric galleries are found in the narrow streets of the old Istrian and Dalmatian towns and villages, particularly Rovinj, Grožnjan and Dubrovnik. Larger galleries can be found in Zagreb.

Natural objects

Practical items such as simple wooden bowls, platters and other carved objects, wickerwork baskets and woven carpets,

---

LOOK BEFORE YOU EAT

Paprenjak are traditional gingerbread hearts given as gifts by lovers. They date back to the Renaissance. Today the edible type can still be bought, but you will also find ceramic or glass versions, decorated with the words 'Croatia' or 'Zagreb'.

all make excellent souvenirs. The local market is often the best place to buy.

Dried lavender and lavender oil can be found in many places along the coast, but it is a particular speciality of Hvar.

LUCKY FOR WHOM?

Rijeka is famed for its lucky mascot, the *morčić*, a miniature bust of a Moor complete with turban. Traditionally it is made of gold and precious stones and sold in pairs to be worn as earrings. The practice is thought to have arisen when the Ottomans were defeated and driven from the city. As a thank-you to the women of Rijeka for their help, their menfolk commissioned small likenesses of the enemy to be worn as a trophy. The *morčić* is now a symbol of the city and is incorporated into many souvenir products.

A la mode

Since the cessation of hostilities, the *fashionistas* have come out in force across Croatia and the streets of all the major towns offer excellent boutiques. Young Croats watch the trends keenly and an evening stroll around the squares in Zagreb or along the waterfront at Rovinj or Split offers the opportunity for a show of style. Image Haddad was founded in 1988 and their simple elegant designs were an instant favourite with prosperous young Croatian women. They now have 18 stores across the country – in all the major towns – plus a second line labelled H2. Heruc Galerija (*www.herucgalerija.hr*) offers Croatian-designed couture at reasonable prices. They have stores in Zagreb, Rijeka,

THE CRAVAT

During the wars of the 17th century, Croatian cavalrymen took to wearing a scarf tied in a unique and distinctive way to help them identify each other on the battlefield. This was much admired, particularly by the French troops, who began to wear their scarves 'in the Croatian style' or 'à la cravate', creating a fashion classic.

Opatija, Zadar and Pula. The current London fashion scene is also graced by Croatian talent as native Vanya Štrok is one half of the Gharani Strok (*www.gharanistrok.co.uk*) up-market label worn by Madonna, Kate Moss and Keira Knightley. Gharani Strok opened their first boutique in Zagreb in March 2005.

Where to spend your money

Most resort towns will have a tourist market, often on the seafront (such as at Opatija) or around the harbour (at Krk Town). This is where the mass-produced items can be found. However, handmade items can also be bought, and the following is a list of established shops or artists recommended for their quality.

An embroidery stall in Dubrovnik

Dubrovnik

Art Studio Renaissance
Artist's studio with offerings on canvas, wood or glass.
Prijeko 21. Tel, mob: (091) 202 5605.

Bokar
Evocative originals and prints concentrating on scenes of Dubrovnik.
Od Puča 20. Tel: (020) 323 271; www.galarija-bokar.hr

Dubrovčka Kuća
Old Dubrovnik house now converted to a gallery selling local handicrafts, wines, olive oils and other souvenirs.
Sv Dominika. Tel: (020) 322 092.

The Ronchi Shop
The Ronchi family have been making hats here since 1858. A unique gift or souvenir.
Lučarica 2. Tel: (020) 323 699.

Grožnjan

Galerija Jedan Plus
Handmade ceramics by artist Mirjana Rajković.
Vincenta iz Kastva 3. Tel: (052) 776 354.

La Giara
Gallery of artist Pamela Ivanković with 'Murano'-style glass creations.
Piazza Paladin Istra. Tel: (052) 776 139.

Hvar

Peko's Gallery
Excellent small boutique on the harbour front.
Hvar Town. Tel: (021) 742 530.

Korčula

Korčula Wind
Great gallery in Venetian tower, full of individual art, handicrafts and gifts.
*Sv Barbare 12, Korčula Town.
Tel: (020) 715 909.*

Opatija

Morsko Blago
Designer jewellery using coral and semi-precious stones. Also modern *morčić*.
M Tita 93/7. Tel: (051) 272 872.

Osijek

Prodavonica
Has a good range of traditional Osijek embroidery plus lace and traditional costumes.
Županijska 15. Tel: (031) 212 217.

TAX REFUNDS

In Croatia it is possible for tourists to receive a refund of VAT (currently 22 per cent) on all goods exported from the country if you spend at least 500kn in one shop. You must have a tax refund form filled out in the shop, and this must be stamped when you leave the country. You must return this form within one year with appropriate bank account details and the refund will be automatically credited.

An artist at work

Poreč
Gold Line
The best range of jewellery in the town, with traditional gold and silver filigree and exceptional amber pieces.
Decumanus 17. Tel: (052) 431 541.

Pula
Zigante
A comprehensive range of Istrian foodstuffs such as preserved truffles, jams, wines and grappas. There are also Zigante shops in Buzet, Umag, Buje and Grožnjan
(*www.zigantetartufi.com*).
Smareglina 7. Tel: (052) 214 855.

Šibenik
Cromovens
On the cathedral square, this shop sells a large range of good-quality souvenirs.
*Trg Republike Hrvatska 4.
Tel: (022) 212 515.*

Split
Split market
The underground vaults of Diocletian's Palace host a craft market with various different products.
No phone.
Studio Naranča
Designer posters, T-shirts and gifts – rather 'arty'.
Majstora Jurja 5. Tel: (021) 344 118.

Varaždin
Gift Shop Nela
Nela Kezelj is a renowned ceramicist and produces excellent *raku* pottery and also sells a range of other handicrafts.
Uska 1. Tel: (042) 215 099.

Zadar
Gallery Pia
Range of goods made by local Zadar and Dalmatian artists and artisans.
Jadro 9. Tel: (023) 251 460.
Kavana Central
Fleamarket selling unusual items.
Široka 3. No phone.

Zagreb
Croata
The best-known producers of the cravat, Croata have a wide range in traditional and modern patterns.
*Kaptol 13. Tel: (01) 481 4600;
www.croata.hr*
Galerija Lav
Upmarket gallery close to Markov trg, showcasing the best in modern Croatian painting, ceramics and sculpture.
Opatička 2. Tel: (01) 492 2108.
Galerija Klovicevi Dvori
Set in Lotrščak Tower, this gallery has a combination of art, sculpture and mass-produced souvenirs.
*Kula Lotrščak, Strossmayerovo
Šetalište 9. Tel: (01) 485 1768;
www.galerijaklovic.hr*
Rodić Ozimec
Award-winning jewellery designer who creates individual modern pieces with precious and semi-precious metals and stones.
Bakačeva 11. Tel: (01) 481 4937.

Entertainment

The genteel pastimes of the Habsburg or Venetian court still resonate around Croatia in the form of a wealth of classical musical performances. These are concentrated during the summer along the coast and the other three seasons in the capital. Theatre also features strongly, following the building of a rash of new auditoria during the late 19th century. For more modern entertainment, you'll find throbbing clubs and discos, plus many casinos for a little (or large) flutter.

THEATRE AND THE ARTS

The Croatian National Theatre now runs a number of auditoria around the country. These have seasonal programmes, often in Croatian, but also including classical performances, opera and ballet.

Orchestral and musical performances transcend language barriers, and the summer is filled with concerts at marvellous venues including St Donat's Church in Zadar, the Rector's Palace in Dubrovnik, or the Cathedral at Varaždin. More conventional venues include the following.

Dubrovnik
Kazalište Marina Držića (Marin Držić Theatre)
There are summer and winter programmes of mainly Croatian drama, held in this pretty theatre dating from 1864.
Pred Dvorum 1. Tel: (020) 321 419; www.kazaliste-dubrovnik.hr

Pag
Centre for Culture
Summer season of plays, opera and exhibitions at various venues around the island.
Od Špitala 2. Tel: (023) 611 025.

Pula
Istre narodno kazalište (National Theatre of Istria)
Hosts film, music and various visual arts performances and exhibitions.
Laginjina 5. Tel: (052) 222 380.

Rovinj
Kazalište Gandusio (Gandusio Theatre)
A year-round varied programme.
Valdibora 17. Tel: (052) 811 588.

Šibenik
Kazalište Šibenik (Theatre Šibenik)
Varied programme throughout the year.
Kralja Zvonimira 1. Ticket office tel: (022) 212 989.

Split

Hrvatsko narodno kazalište (Croatian National Theatre)

A full range of domestic and international drama, ballet and opera.
Trg Gaje Bulata 1. Tel: (021) 344 999; www.hnk-split.hr

Varaždin

Hrvatsko narodno kazalište (Croatian National Theatre)

Hosts Baroque evenings during the summer and Festival of Baroque nights in September/October. Also home to the Varaždin Chamber Orchestra.
Augusta Cesarca 1. Tel: (042) 214 688, ticket office (042) 212 907; www.vko.hr

Zadar

Hrvatska Kazališna Kuća (Croatian Theatre House)

Runs a full summer festival, with concerts also in St Donat's Church.
Široka 8. Tel: info (023) 300 430, tickets (023) 314 586.

The flagship Croatian National Theatre in Zagreb

Zagreb

Concertna dvorana Vatroslav Lisinski (Vatroslav Lisinski Concert Hall)

Home to the Zagreb Philharmonic and host to major orchestras from around the world. The small hall hosts ensembles and virtuoso performances.
Trg Stjepana Radica 4. Tel: (01) 612 1166; www.lisinski.hr
Ticket office open: Mon–Fri 9am–8pm, Sat 9am–2pm.

Dramsko Kazalište Gavella (Gavella Drama Theatre)

International and Croatian theatre.
Frankopanska 8. Tel: (01) 4849 222; www.gavella.hr
Ticket office daily 10am–1pm & 5.30–7.30pm.

Gradsko Kazalište Komedija (Municipal Comedy Theatre)

Performances in Croatian, and international hits such as *Little Shop of Horrors.*
Kaptol 9. Tel: (01) 481 4566; www.komedija.hr
Ticket office open 90 min before performances.

Hrvatski glazbeni zavod (The Croatian Music Institute)

Classical ensembles and academy performances, chamber music, etc.
Gunduliceva 6. Tel: (01) 483 0822.
Ticket office open: Mon–Fri 11am–1pm and one hour before performances.

Hrvatsko narodno kazalište (Croatian National Theatre)

A full range of domestic and international drama, ballet and opera.

The Meštrović Gallery in Vrpolje

Trg maršala Tita 15. Tel: (01) 482 2532;
www.hnk.hr
Ticket office Mon–Fri 10am–2pm,
Sat–Sun 30 min before performances.

Off Theatre Bagatella
Cutting-edge performances, master
classes and recitations. All
performances in Croatian.
Bednjanska 13. Tel: (01) 617 0423.
Ticket office open: daily 4–6pm.

Satiričko Kazalište Kerempuh
(Kerempuh Satirical Theatre)
Theatre performances in Croatian only,
but also hosts regular magic acts.
Also holds night theatre cabaret
commencing at 11pm.
Ilica 31. Tel: (01) 483 3347.
Ticket office open: Tue–Sun 10am–noon
and 10am–11pm on performance days.

Teatar ITD (ITD Theatre)
Avant-garde performances and small-
scale festivals.
Savska cesta 25. Tel: (01) 484 3492.
Ticket office open: Mon–Sat 10am–1pm
and 2 hours prior to performance.

In addition to individual theatre ticket
offices, there is a communal ticket office
at Oktogon, Ilica 5. Tel: (01) 4810 909.
Open: Mon–Fri 11am–7pm, Sat
10am–2pm.

NIGHTCLUBS AND DISCOS

There's a thriving club and disco scene
in Zagreb and in the other major cities;
this extends along the coast during the
summer season. Most major hotels have
discos, but be aware that these will be
very seasonal and perhaps lacking in
atmosphere in May or September. In the
north and east, discothèques and clubs
give way to café bars that play music on
summer nights or at weekends during
the winter. We've included a list of
major clubs, discos and bars in some
cities, and large hotel clubs.

Brač
Faces
Favourite spot on the island close to
Zlatni rat beach.
Gorje Podbarje, Bol.
Tel: (021) 635 920.

Dubrovnik
Disco Club Orsetta
Set in the catacombs of the Revelin
Fort. There's an open-air terrace so you
can dance outside.
Tvrđava Revelin. Sv Dominika.
Tel: (020) 322 164.

Labirint
One of the most fashionable spots in
the Old Town.
Svetog Dominika. Tel: (020) 322 222.

Hvar

Carpe Diem

Large open-air club with an international reputation.
Riva, Hvar Town. Tel: (021) 717 234.

Opatija

Note: all Opatija's clubs close during the winter months.

Camelia, Grand Hotel Adriatic

Music from the 1970s through to the latest club anthems.
Tel: (051) 719 000.

Pag

Aquarius

In summer Aquarius sets up a fantastic open-air party space here. It's the best clubbing scene in Croatia.
Zrće Beach, Novalja. No phone, but in winter see details for Aquarius Zagreb on p158.

Poreč

Atalier 1

Multimedia centre with music, multiscreens and Internet access.
Obala M Tita 3A. Tel: (098) 951 8307.

International Club

Large complex that draws an international tourist crowd.
Zelena Laguna. Tel: (052) 451 392.

Rijeka

Teuta Club/café bar

Café-bar that converts to music venue in the evenings (although not every evening).
Užarska 1. Tel: (051) 335 712.

Split

Tribu

Disco café-bar with open-air dance area – busiest on summer weekends.
Osmih Mediteranskih igara 3. Tel: (021) 322 477; www.clubtribu.com

Tropic Club Equador

A hip café-bar that turns club later in the evening.
Kupaliste Bavcica. Tel: (021) 323 571; www.tropic-club-equador.com

Trogir

Monaco Disco Bar

Just across the bridge from town on Čiovo waterfront, this large bar turns disco on summer evenings.
Kraj Zvonimir 7. No phone.

Varaždin

Rock Art Café

This disco stays open after all the others close, so it tends to get very full in the early hours.
Preradovićeva 24. Tel: (042) 321 123.

A busker draws a crowd

Zadar

Arsenal

The old Venetian waterfront arsenal has been converted into a fashionable multi-use space including a cool bar/club for late evenings.
Trg tri bunara. Tel: (023) 253 833;
www.arsenalzadar.com

Corso

Popular bar with disco on summer weekends. Pleasant terrace for dancing away the summer nights.
Mihovila Pavlinovića 4.
Tel: (098) 182 7741.

Zagreb

With a large young and trend-conscious population, as well as a student contingent, Zagreb has numerous nightclubs. These form the tip of the iceberg:

Aquarius

Probably the best club in Zagreb, known throughout Croatia as 'the place to be'. Guest DJs and live performances. Transfers to the island of Pag during the summer (*see p157*).
Matje Ljubeka bb, Jarun. Tel: (01) 364 0231; www.aquarius.hr

Boogaloo

The famed OTV Club has been given a revamp – this is the place for serious clubbing.
Vukovarska 68, 13. Tel: (01) 6313 021.

BP-Jazz Club

All kinds of jazz, including live performances. Hosts a jazz convention each autumn.
Teslina 7. Tel: (01) 481 4444.

KINO (CINEMA)

Films are shown in original language with Croatian subtitles, so you can watch the Hollywood blockbusters here. Zagreb and the major cities have multiscreen complexes, but they are not common in smaller towns. You may also find in smaller cinemas that they don't show the latest releases, but if you've enjoyed it once, why not revisit a favourite?

Dubrovnik

Kino Sloboda

Luža 1. Tel: (020) 321 425.

Porec

Kino Poreč

Narodni trg 1. Tel: (052) 453 599.

Trogir

Kino Domobran

Dr Franje Tuđmana 2A.
Tel (021) 881 975

Zadar

Kino Zadar

Široka ulica. Tel: (023) 251 034.

Cinema houses are often small and traditional

Zagreb

The following cinemas dish up strictly Hollywood fodder:

Broadway Kino
Centar Kaptol, Nova Ves 11. Tel: (01) 466 7686; www.broadway-kina.com

Cinestar
Branimirova 29. Tel: (01) 468 6600; www.blitz-cinestar.hr

CASINOS

A very popular leisure pastime in Croatia, casinos make an interesting way to pass a few hours – provided you don't lose your shirt. Opening times tend to be around 4pm, with most not closing until 6am. Dress codes apply at most casinos.

Dubrovnik
Casino Miro, Hotel Excelsior
Frane Supila 12. Tel: (020) 312 077; www.casinomiro.com

Fireworks light up Dubrovnik

Opatija
Grand Hotel Adriatic
M Tita 200. Tel: (051) 719 182.

Poreč
Casino Hotel Parentium
Zelena Laguna. Tel: (052) 411 500.

Pula
Casino Histria
Hotel Histria, Verudela. Tel: (052) 590 000.

Umag
Casino Umag
On the seafront next to the Hotel Kristal.
Obala M Tita 7. Tel: (052) 743 453.

Zadar
Casino Zadar
*Ivana Mažuranića b.b.
Tel: (023) 239 410.*

Zagreb
Club Casino Vega
*Draskoviceva 43 (at the Hotel Sheraton).
Tel: (01) 4553 535.*

Four Points Casino
*Four Points Sheraton Panorama Hotel.
Tel: (01) 3658 333.*

International
There are no gambling tables here but only games machines.
Miramarska cesta 24. Tel: (01) 3637 399.

Children

Though there are few activities or attractions specifically designed for children, Croatia certainly has plenty to offer. It will appeal especially to active older children (8+) who love being outdoors.

Beach activities

Croatian waters are some of the cleanest in Europe. They are crystal-clear and usually calm in summer – perfect for swimming and snorkelling. Or try your hand at windsurfing, kayaking and water-skiing – they are guaranteed to tire out even the most energetic child.

One word of caution when booking your holiday: many Croatian beaches consist of pebbles not sand, and entry to the water is often from a lido rather than from the beach. Though this isn't a problem for older children and those who can swim, it may not suit very young children who want to build sandcastles and play in the shallows. Make enquiries about exact beach conditions with the tourist office before making your booking.

Sports and outdoor pursuits

The mountain-biking, cycling and hiking/rambling possibilities are seemingly endless. For children with cycling proficiency the islands make perfect places for exploration, and cycle hire is easy and cheap. There are many safe marked tracks (particularly good at Zlatni Rt in Rovinj – *see p146*), and in the national and nature parks. If they want to try something more adventurous, then introductory sessions for climbing and abseiling are good fun. For details of organisations who run the above activities, *see pp163–5*.

Horse-riding

Trekking is popular, and most stables cater to all abilities. Treks can last from a couple of hours to a whole day (with lunch) and offer a slower-paced way to see a little of the Croatian countryside. Lessons are also usually available, but not all instructors speak English. Konjički centar Libertas at the Holiday Village Zaton offers a full riding-lessons service.

Konjički centar Libertas, Holiday Village Zaton, Nin (north of Zadar). Tel: (098) 472 227; www.horse-center-libertas.hr

Boat trips

Most children love getting out onto the water and there is a wide choice of day-trips from almost anywhere on the coast: great for filling a day or two. Full-day organised trips always offer lunch, and usually time for swimming too. For further details on boat trips on offer *see pp168–9*. For something more unusual, try heading under the water in a mini-submarine to get a closer look at the marine life.

The Yellow Submarine, Port, Poreč. Tel: (098) 229 573.

Festivals

The full diary of summer festivals always offers something for children, be it parades with traditional costumes, Croatian song and dance, jousting contests, religious processions or old-fashioned funfair 'games of chance'. The major festivals and events for the whole country are listed on *pp26–7*, but this is only the tip of the iceberg and there are numerous other smaller fairs in each region for you to enjoy. Consult your local tourist office when you get to Croatia to find out what's going on.

Theatre

Zagreb has a number of performance venues specifically for children where the language barrier shouldn't cause too many difficulties for non-Croatian kids.

Dubrava Children's Theatre

Cerska 1. Tel: (01) 291 0487.

Ribica Children's Theatre

Ribnjak Park 1. Tel: (01) 481 4734; www.cmr.hr

Zagreb Puppet Theatre

Performances take place in Drustveni dom Tresnjevka.
Stara Trešnjevka 1. Tel: (01) 369 5457.

Zagreb Theatre of the Young

Treslina 7. Tel: (01) 487 2554; www.zekaem.hr

Children

Young girls enjoying the sunshine and clean sea

Sport and leisure

As far as spectator sports are concerned, the organisation of these is still recovering from the effects of the war and many pan-Yugoslav activities have yet to recommence. But if you want to play sports yourself, there are lots of opportunities in Croatia to get out and get active. You can also enjoy some of the best natural landscapes and seascapes in Europe.

SPECTATOR SPORTS

Funding for activities such as athletics is practically nonexistent, but three sports have an important hold on Croatian sporting minds.

Basketball

Basketball has grown massively in the last decade. Cibona Zagreb (*www.cibona.com*) is involved in the Euroleague, an international circuit with teams from across Europe. There's also an Adriatic League; a full domestic league programme takes place with a 14-team A1 league and several lower divisions, including teams from Zadar, Split, Rijeka and Šibenik.

Contact: Croatian Basketball Federation, Lipovečka 1/III, 10110 Zagreb. Tel: (01) 3688 950; fax: (01) 368 8951; www.hks-cbf.hr

For up-to-date information, stats and team and player info, try *www.eurobasket.com*. It's a commercial site but with comprehensive information about the sport.

Football

Like much of the world, football or soccer is by far the most popular spectator sport. Croatians play in top teams across Europe, but the Croatian National League consists of a rather meagre 12 teams. You'll find league clubs at Osijek, Pula, Rijeka and Zadar, with several clubs in the capital Zagreb. *Contact the Croatian Football Federation: Rusanova 13, 10000 Zagreb. Tel: (01) 236 1555; fax: (01) 2441 500; www.hns-cff.hr*

Hadjuk Split's football ground

Reaching a peak at Paklenica National Park

Handball

The success of Croatia's men's handball team (who won gold at the Athens Olympics in 2004) is spurred on by a vibrant domestic league, with clubs in Zagreb, Split, Rijeka and Osijek.
Croatia Handball Federation, Haulikova 6, 10000 Zagreb. Tel: (01) 457 6111; fax: (01) 457 3036.

The official website *www.hrs.hr* has no information in English, so try *www.eurohandball.com* with information about what's happening in Croatia and around Europe.

PARTICIPATION SPORTS

There is a wide range of sports you can practise in Croatia, and for many activities you need neither expertise nor qualifications.

Bird-watching (*see pp98–9*)

Climbing

Croatia has a long history of leisure mountaineering, though it isn't on the sport's top-ten list of destinations. Free climbing is also growing in popularity, but is only permitted in designated areas. The Paklenica National Park (in Dalmatia) is a particularly choice spot, with a range of 400 equipped climbing routes to suit all abilities. Climbers need to buy a separate climbing pass, as park tickets do not include permission to climb. Register with the climbing information book at the park entrance. The park holds international big wall speed-climbing competitions in late April and early May.

Climbing courses are run by the Zlatni Rt Forest Park (*see p146*), and it is possible to climb without guides at the Punta Montauro site.

Baredine provide caving and cave-climbing (descending into caves with ropes) experiences. Or contact ProMontana for more details on their day climbing courses.
Baredine, 52446 Nova Vas, Poreč. Tel: (052) 421 333; www.baredine.com
ProMontana, Marina, Rovinj. Tel: (052) 384 184.

Cycling and mountain biking

The offshore islands are perfect places to take to two wheels. Most regional tourist organisations produce booklets on local routes. The best is a Kvarner Country tourist office booklet entitled

Cycle tours – a great way to see the countryside

'Kvarner by Bicycle'. There is excellent cycling at Zlatni Rt Nature Park (*see p146*), with bike hire on hand, and you can cycle too in the Paklenica National Park, provided that you do not impede hikers, though there are no facilities to rent equipment.

Kvarner Country tourist office, ul Nikole Tesle 2, 51410 Opatija. Tel: (051) 272 988; www.kvarner.hr

Bike rental and tours:

Bol, Brač – *Big Blue Sport (see water sports, right) with bike hire and tours.*

Medulin – *Prematura. Tel: (091) 512 3646; www.windsurfing.hr*

Poreč – *Bike Point B, Parentina 19. Tel: (052) 453 520.*

Pula – *Istraway, Riva 14. Tel: (052) 214 613.*

Zadar – *Eurobike Obala kneza Branimira 6c. Tel: (023) 241 243.*

Diving

The clear waters around Croatia are an excellent place to dive. There is organised

diving in Kornati and Mljet National Parks. Divers' cards are issued by the Croatian Diving Federation and are valid for one year. They will only be issued to those with a suitable diving qualification, though you can also learn to dive here.

Cavtat

Epidaurum

Šetalište Žal b.b., 20210 Cavtat. Tel: (020) 471 386; fax: (020) 471 386; www.epidauum-diving-cavtat.hr

Hvar

Dive Center Viking

Plodstine b.b., 21450 Hvar. Tel: (021) 742 529; www.viking-diving.com

Rab

Moby Dick

Lopar 493, 51281 Rab. Tel: (051) 775 577; www.moby-dick1.com

Zadar

Zadar Sub

Dubrovačka 20a, 23000 Zadar. Tel: (023) 214 848; www.zadarsub.hr

For up-to-date information, consult *www.diving-hrs.hr*

Fishing

Although the Mediterranean fish stock is not as exciting and numerous as the Caribbean's, it is still possible to hook something spectacular – huge bluefin tuna, for example. You will need a licence; the harbour-master's office will tell you where to buy them.

Try Magic Blue Yachting, Supilova 26A, 21000 Split. Tel: (021) 332 332; fax: (021) 332 331; www.magicyachting.com
For a more gentle approach try

river-fishing for trout and other freshwater species. You'll need a licence, normally available from the tourist office.

For fly-fishing on Kupa River and Gacka River in northern Croatia contact Mislav Jukić. Tel: (01) 388 5870; www.kupa-flyfishing.com

Hiking

The Croatian Mountaineering Association maintains footpaths in the mountains (particularly good areas are the Gorski Kotar in Kvarner and the Velebit ranges in northern Dalmatia), and trails are well signposted.

Paklenica National Park in northern Dalmatia has over 150km (94 miles) of marked trails (*see pp141–2*).

A series of footpaths have been created in the north of Cres around Beli, taking walkers past 10 'stations' of natural interest. Routes are of various lengths, starting at 5km (3 miles).

Paklenica National Park. Tel: (023) 369 155; www.paklenica.hr

Sailing (*see pp168–9*)

Spas (*see pp148–9*)

Tennis

The success of Croatian Goran Ivanisević (Wimbledon men's singles champion in 2001) and more recently Mario Ančić and Ivan Ljubičić has encouraged investment in facilities all round the country, and most large

hotels on the coast also have courts. The best is the Tennis Centre at the Sol Melia Hotel in Umag.

Water sports

Provision for most water sports is growing, but it is most prevalent in the large tourist resorts such as Makarska (*see p76*) or Umag (*see p79*). Big Blue Adventure Sport offers windsurfing training and a range of other activities in Bol. Prematura is an excellent Istrian organisation with a windsurfing school that also rents equipment.

Big Blue Sport, Rodan Glavice 2, Bol, Brač. Tel: (021) 635 614; www.big-blue-sport-hr Prematura. Tel: (091) 512 3646; www.windsurfing.hr

TOURIST AGENCIES

Most commercial tourist agencies, or '*biros*', as they are known in Croatia, will be able to book organised sports for you. One of the best is Investigator Tours, who run cycling, fly- and sea-fishing, riding, sea- and river-kayaking, white-water rafting, windsurfing and climbing trips. Investigator Tours, *Mažuranićevo Šetalište 8a, 21000 Split. Tel: (021) 321 698; mobile (098) 168 7749; www.investigator.hr*

SAFETY FIRST

Not all of these activities are covered by the standard travel insurance policy. Please check to make sure you are covered before you start the activity and, if not, make sure that the company operating the activity is insured to cover your costs or repatriate you if you are injured.

Naturism

Naturism is an important element in Croatian tourist provision. The first official naturist beach opened in 1934 on the island of Rab, though the area had earned a certain reputation throughout the Austrian lands from the turn of the 20th century. In 1936 naturism hit the world stage when the Duke of Windsor (King Edward VIII) stayed here, swimming naked in the Bay of Kandarola; but it was in the 1960s that naturist resorts really took off.

Today there are more than 30 official naturist tourist resorts, with accommodation (often self-catering cottages and camping sites),

The official naturism sign

entertainment and sporting facilities. Here you can enjoy the freedom of life in the nude, surrounded by like-minded people. Naturist resorts now offer almost 47,000 camping places and 6,000 hotel beds.

Many campsites are divided into sections, with areas for naturists and areas for 'textiles' (as naturists call those who like to wear clothes). Clothing must be worn in communal areas such as bars or shops (though it may only be a bikini or swimming trunks), but in the fully naturist areas, nudity is the norm.

Outside these resorts there are numerous 'clothing optional' beaches where nudists and textiles share the sand. To avoid embarrassment, the beaches are usually loosely segregated into a textile section and a nude section. Nudists would not be expected to venture into the textile areas fully naked, but if you want to wear a swimming costume yet still sunbathe in the nudist section, that's perfectly acceptable.

Official naturist beaches are clearly marked with the FKK sign. This stands for the German 'Freikörperkultur', which translates as 'free body culture', but such is Croatia's reputation within the naturist/nudist

There are plenty of secluded beaches in Croatia

world that you are likely to find people sunbathing nude on any remote beach or tiny cove.

Most exponents are discreet and won't want to cause offence, but if you really find nudism offensive then your best bet is to stick to the main town beaches in the resorts where Croatian families go, as they generally aren't fond of disrobing.

What is naturism?

Naturism is often thought of as simply taking your clothes off on the beach, but in its true sense it implies nudity within social settings, not as a form of blatant exhibitionism but as a way of getting back to a simpler way of life. It was often expounded as part of a holistic approach to life, to balance mind and body.

Naturism as a lifestyle was developed in Germany in the post-Victorian era, perhaps as a contrast to the very constrained and formal attitudes and moral codes that had developed in the late 19th century.

Naturist decorum

Here's what to do and what not to do when in a naturist area or resort.

1. Make sure that the beach is a nudist beach. If you don't see the FKK sign, look around at your fellow bathers. If you are not sure, find a quiet, remote part of the beach before going completely nude.

2. Sit on a towel when on public benches or invited to join others around a table. Always carry a towel for this purpose.

3. Only photograph nude people with their permission.

4. No overt sexual activity in public – many families are naturists and it is not considered seemly.

www.cronatur.com is the best website for information on naturism in Croatia.

Sailing

The magnificent coastline and innumerable offshore islands combined with benign summer waters make Croatia one of the prime sailing destinations in the world. Ports are well organised for the yachting crowd and there is a multitude of companies offering boat rental, package trips or crewed boats for those with or without Day Skipper certificates.

A popular choice for beginners, or those wanting a social trip, is the flotilla holiday. This involves groups of boats sailing together on a set route, usually with a guide. The most popular routes for flotillas are around Trogir, Korčula and Dubrovnik in the south of the country, combining the sailing with plenty of sites of historical and cultural interest as soon as you step off the boat.

If you have a Day Skipper certificate (*see below*), you'll be allowed to take a boat out yourself. With the wind in your sails you can wend your way to that remote cove you've pinpointed on your chart.

Catching the breeze

for boats, shower facilities and even accommodation. The most romantic are those where you can disembark and sit on the quayside enjoying an aperitif, or dine at a restaurant overlooking the yachts. You'll pay a daily fee for services and mooring.

Marinas

Marinas in Croatia vary in size and in their facilities. The most basic offer berths and fresh water, whilst the most modern will have electrical hook-ups

Popular ports of call

Bol or **Cavtat** for their small picturesque harbours (*see p74 and p100*).

The **Kornati Islands National Park** is a favourite destination among independent sailors because there are very few other people around (*see pp139–40*).

Rovinj, for its wonderful atmosphere and evening *passeggiata* (*see p57*).

Split has a huge marina where the Croatian jet-setters meet at weekends (*see p84*).

From **Trogir** you can walk direct into the old town (*see p86*).

The following companies have a good deal of experience in holiday provision for both flotilla and bareboat yachting:

Neilson

Locksview, Brighton Marina, Brighton, BN2 5HA, UK. Tel: 0870 333 3356; fax: 0870 909 9089; www.neilson.co.uk

Sunsail

The Port House, Port Solent, Portsmouth, Hampshire, PO6 4TH. Tel: (02392) 222222; fax: (02392) 219827; www.sunsail.com

For luxury yacht charter, try Navis Yacht Charter, 145–157 St John Street, London EC1V 4PY. Tel: 07941 466507; www.navis-yacht-charter.com

Boats at anchor

The Day Skipper certificate

This card allows 'the skipper' to be responsible for the safety of his/her boat and crew for sailing in daylight only, in local waters (not too far from the shore, not out in the open ocean), requiring only basic navigational skills, in moderate wind and sea conditions.

Crosail offer one-day, one-night and one-week courses for all abilities. It's a great way to discover if the ocean life is for you.

Crosail, Bukovačka 73, 10000 Zagreb. Tel: (01) 242 1738; www.crosail.com

Useful organisations

The Adriatic Croatia International Club (ACI) is the leading provider of marina facilities, boat rental and crews in Croatia. Joining their organisation will give you discounts on berthing fees at their 21 modern marinas along the Croatian coast. The Croatia Tourist Organisation produces a booklet entitled 'Information for Sailors', which lays out the rules and regulations for all boaters in Croatian waters, including radio frequencies, marina telephone numbers and charter organisations. It's available from official tourist offices, or via their website.

Adriatic Croatia International Club (ACI); www.aci-club.hr
Croatia Tourist Organisation; www.croatia.hr

Food and drink

As one might expect given Croatia's history, Austro-Hungarian country cuisine mixes with Italian influences on the coast; even some Ottoman Turkish methods still linger. Today there is a real geographical divide between the coast and inland Croatia in the types and range of food on offer.

Appetisers

Stuffed cabbage leaves (*sarma*) reveal Croatia's Ottoman heritage, while the vegetable soup (*manistra*) is closely related to the Italian *minestrone*. You'll also find plates of the ubiquitous sheep's cheese from Pag (*paški sir*), Dalmatian ham (*Dalmatinski pršut*) or spicy paprika sausage (*kulen*).

Main courses

Seafood dominates the coast, and is exceptionally fresh and delicious. Fish (*riba*) is often served simply grilled, or try octopus, mussels or oysters.

Kebabs (*ražnijići*) and small sausages (*Čevapčići*) make tasty and cheap meals. Mixed grill is popular; you will also see whole carcasses of young pig or lamb, slowly turning over hot coals.

Inland, where winters are longer and colder, food tends to be more substantial. The influence of Austro-Hungary is plainly seen with the predominance of paprika as a flavouring. Here your *manistra*

becomes *jota*: it has the same base of vegetables but includes heartier ingredients such as pulses. The famous Hungarian meat stew *goulash* makes an appearance here too, along with a fresh fish stew (*fiš paprikaš*). Large pasta parcels (*štruckli*) are baked in the oven: they have savoury fillings for a main course or sweet fillings for dessert.

Desserts

Štrudel is more often filled with nuts and honey than apple. Try *rozata*, a crème caramel with a dash of bitter liqueur, or *palačinka* (filled pancakes). Ice cream (*sladoled*) is a favourite with Croatians, and is produced in a delicious range of flavours.

What to drink

You'll find excellent coffee (*kava*) all across Croatia. Tea, local mineral water and fruit juices are widely available.

For something a little stronger, try domestically brewed beer (*pivo*). Karlovačko and Ožujsko are the most common lagers. Local wine is of good quality, and the stronger liqueurs such as the plum brandy *sljivovica* and grape-based *rakia/grappa* are excellent. Both *Travarica* and *Pelinkovac* are herb-based spirits.

Food for thought – vegetarians

Vegetarians will have few difficulties in Croatia, but vegans will struggle to find variety when eating out.

Inland, the cuisine staples all include portions of meat, and many of the vegetable soups served may have a base of meat stock, so ask before ordering.

Recommended restaurants

The price ranges below are per person, for a three-course meal without wine. Restaurants are generally more expensive on the coast and in Zagreb than in the rest of the country.

£	under 200kn
££	200–250kn
£££	250–300kn
££££	over 300kn

WHERE TO EAT AND DRINK

Though the differences between these eateries are beginning to blur, these descriptions should still be useful.

Bife – snack bar

Estoran – formal restaurant

Gostionica – informal, taverna-style eatery

Kavana – café serving alcoholic and non alcoholic drinks

Konoba – traditional wine bars offering local dishes on a limited menu

Pivnica – beer hall

Slasticarna – pastry cafés and ice-cream emporia serving drinks but not alcohol

PRICES

Many restaurants, particularly in eastern Croatia, price fish and meat by the kilo and drinks by the full bottle, rather than by portion size. This can cause confusion, but the staff will always be helpful if you ask.

Cres

Konoba Riva £

This fish restaurant is attached to the fish market, so you can't get any fresher than that. Simple tables and décor.

Riva creskih kapetana 13, Cres Town. Tel: (051) 571 107. Closed Nov–Mar.

Dubrovnik

Nautika ££££

Elegant dining with fine cuisine using the best local ingredients – seafood predominates.

Brsalje 3. Tel: (020) 442 526.

Preparing a pig for spit-roasting in Poreč

Food and drink

Hum

Humska Konoba ££

Tiny restaurant with shaded terrace and lovely views over the central Istrian countryside.
Hum.
Tel: (052) 660 005. Closed Nov–Mar, Mon–Fri.

Hvar

L'Antica £

Beloved of the glitterati, this is the place to be seen, where everyone meets for aperitifs.
Stari Grad.
Tel: (098) 171 7491.

Na po ure £

Good-value, modern *konobo* with excellent barrel wines.
Špire Brusine 8.
Tel: (023) 312 004.

Alfresco dining is the norm

Livade (Istria)

Zigante Tartufi ££££

Voted top restaurant in Croatia in 2005, Zigante Tartufi is a gastronomic delight and uses ample amounts of the truffles for which they are famed.
Levade 7.
Tel: (052) 664 302;
www.zigantetartufi.com

Pula

Kunskafe Cvajner £

Arts café with live music and fresco-covered walls.
Forum 2.
Tel: (052) 420 401

Valsabbion ££££

Consistently one of the very best restaurants in Croatia.
Pješčana ulava IX/26.
Tel: (052) 222 991.

Rab

Konoba Rab ££

Rustic-style eatery serving traditional *peka* stews. Other dishes are also available.
Kneza Branimira 3, Rab Town. Tel: (051) 725 666. Closed Nov–early Feb.

Rovinj

Kanoba Veli Jože ££

Well-established restaurant in the old town. Fish and Istrian specialities are on offer.
Ul Svetob Križa 3.
Tel: (052) 816 337.

Valentino Wine Bar £

Ultra-fashionable wine bar with seats on the waterfront rocks and submerged lights for after-dark atmosphere.
Ul Svetob Križa 24.
Tel: (052) 816 334.

Split

Enoteka Terra ££

Stone Croatian wine cellar serving 'tapas'-style snacks.
Brače Kaliterne 6.
Tel: (021) 314 800.

Restoran Nostromo ££££

Award-winning new fish restaurant. It's pricy but great for an excellent lunch or dinner.
Kraj Sv Marije 10.
Tel: (091) 405 6666; www.restoran-nostromo.hr

Ston

Bota Šare ££

Overlooking the harbour at Mali Ston, housed in a 14th-century arsenal store. Seafood and traditional cuisine.
Mali Ston.
Tel: (020) 754 482.

Café-bars on the pavements are abundant

Trogir
Mirina Capo ££
One of many atmospheric rustic eateries in town.
Ribarska 11.
Tel: (021) 885 334;
www.capo-trogir.com

Varaždin
Varaždin ££
Four kilometres
(2¹/₂ miles) out of town by a man-made lake, this is one of Croatia's top 100 restaurants, serving local cuisine.
Aquacity, Međimurska 26.
Tel: (042) 350 555.

Veliki Tabor
Grešna Gorica £
An excellent example of a family-owned rustic taverna.
Veliki Tabor.
Tel: (049) 434 001;
www.gresna-gorica.com

Volosko (near Opatija)
Le Mandrać £££–££££
A chic glass-sided dining area, Le Mandrać offers a contrast to the traditional architecture of Volosko fishing village. Menu concentrates on traditional dishes and has received Gault Mallau accreditation.
Obala F Supila 10.
Tel: (051) 701 357;
www.lemandrac.com

Zadar
Arsenal ££–£££
Ultra-modern eatery in this refurbished complex dating from the 18th century. The menu brings influences from around the world.
Trg tri bunara 1.
Tel: (023) 253 833;
www.arsenalzadar.com

Kornat £££
One of the best places to eat in the old town. Traditional dishes are given a new twist.
Liburnska obala 6.
Tel: (023) 254 501.

Zagreb
Ivica i Marica £
A popular restaurant with the young and fashionable, this gingerbread-styled eatery serves excellent crêpes and ice cream.
Tkalčićeva 70.
Tel: 01 482 8999;
www.ivicaimarica.com
Kerempuh £££
Regarded as the best fish restaurant in the capital with views over the activity of Dolac market.
Kaptol 3.
Tel: (01) 481 9000;
www.kerempuh.hr
Okrugljak ££££
One of the best restaurants in Zagreb.
Mlinovi 28, Sljeme (Medvednica).
Tel: (01) 467 4112.
Vinodol ££££
Wonderful brick-domed dining room with a small terrace.
Teslina 10. Tel: (01) 481 1427; www.vinodol-zg.hr

Hotels and accommodation

Croatia has a good range of accommodation, but the vast majority of it is found along the coastal strip, on the islands, and in Zagreb. At the moment there is ample accommodation provision, except during the peak season (late July to end August), when it is important to make a firm booking, especially at coastal locations.

Hotels

Many hotels date from the 1980s; although most were renovated in the late 1990s, it's worth checking that is the case. Hotels in mansions, castles and other historic properties are likely to cost more.

Hotels are rated in one of five categories, according to government criteria. L, A and B – the upper categories – must have private facilities in each room. However, an increasing number of hotels use the more widely understood 'star' rating system. Motels can be found on major road routes.

Room rates are generally a little below what you would expect to pay for the equivalent in Western Europe. Pricing for rooms varies according to the season and facilities. The highest rates apply late July to late August.

Rented rooms and self-catering accommodation

Rented rooms (*sobe*) and self-catering accommodation (*apartman*) are well developed. These are vetted by the tourist authorities and divided into three star categories, the highest of which (3 stars) must have private bathroom facilities for each room.

Tourist offices should keep a list of local self-catering and private room accommodation. Women often offer rooms to rent at the ferry port; failing that, signs in windows usually indicate rooms or apartments for rent. Private rooms are around one-third the price of a basic hotel room.

Camping

The Croatian coastline is one of the best places in Europe for camping provision, with more than 140 campsites of varying sizes. Almost all are found close to the coast or around Krka or Plitvice National Parks (*see pp140 and 143*). There are no campsites in the east as yet, but this should change as visitor numbers grow. Zagreb has one campsite affiliated to the Plitvice Motel on the outskirts of the city at the service station on the A1/E59 motorway, hence it's noisy. Be aware that some are naturist facilities (*see pp166–7*), so check beforehand.

The Croatia Tourist Board website *www.croatia.hr* has comprehensive information on camping and campsites, or visit *www.camping.hr*, the home page of the Croatian Camping Union.

Most campsites are closed from October until April.

Agrotourism

This fast-growing sector of the market offers bed and breakfast or self-catering accommodation in the country, on a farm or in a village house. Check with the Croatia Tourist Board.

Hostels

The Croatian Youth Hostel Association (*www.hfhs.hr*) operates hostels in seven locations around the country in Dubrovnik, Pula, Punat, Rijeka, Veli Lošinj, Zadar and Zagreb. Accommodation depends on the individual hostel as these vary in size from 60 beds to 210 beds – some have

The Hotel Adriatic at Rovinj

private rooms and some have family rooms. Booking is essential in high season. Contact the association for more details. The website is an excellent source of information.
Savska 5/1, 10000 Zagreb.
Tel: (01) 482 9294.

SUGGESTED HOTELS

Price are for a double room without breakfast in peak season.

£	under 600kn
££	600–1,000kn
£££	1,000–1,500kn
££££	over 1,500kn

Cavtat
Hotel Supetar ££
Cosy small hotel on the harbour front.
Obala A Starčevića 27, 20210 Cavtat.
Tel: (020) 479 833; fax: (020) 479 858.

Dubrovnik
Pucić Palace ££££
Exceptional five-star boutique hotel – a renovated mansion in the old town.
Od Puča 1, 2000 Dubrovnik. Tel: (020) 326 200; www.thepucicpalace.com

Hvar
Riva Hotel ££££
This new luxury hotel set in a century-old warehouse has been getting excellent press reviews around Europe. Great location next to the yacht harbour, and a contemporary interior.
Riva, 21450 Hvar. Tel: (021) 750 100; fax: (021) 750 101; www.suncanihvar.com

The Hotel Mozart at Opatija

Mali Lošinj
Hotel Apoksiomen £££
This stunning waterfront property is now a chic hotel and café bar – very unusual in the islands.
Riva Lošinjskih kapetena I, Mali Lošinj, 51550 Lošinj. Tel: (051) 520 820; fax: (051) 520 830; www.apoksiomen.com

Opatija
Hotel Mozart £££
Bijou refurbished five-star hotel across the road from the seafront promenade.
M Tita 138, 51410 Opatija. Tel: (051) 718 260; www.hotel-mozart.hr

Osijek
Hotel Osijek £££
This new glass tower dominates the waterfront at the heart of Osijek, providing a social centre for a downtown area.
Šamaćka 4, 31000 Osijek. Tel: (031) 230 330; fax: (031) 230444; www.hotelosijek.hr

Rijeka
Grand Hotel Bonavia ££
Grand hotel with luxury fittings and excellent service.
Dolac 4, 51000 Rijeka. Tel: (051) 357 100; fax: (051) 335 969; www.bonavia.hr

Rovinj
Hotel Adriatic ££
Perfectly placed on the harbourside. Simple but comfortable rooms, some with three beds.
Trg Budicin bb, 52210 Rovinj. Tel: (052) 815 088; www.maistra.hr

Slavonski Brod
Zdjelarević ££
Small hotel set within a private winery about 10km (6 miles) west of Slavonski Brod. Excellent restaurant and a sauna.
Vinogradska 102, 35253 Bronski Stupnik. Tel: (035) 427 775; fax: (035) 427 040.

Split
Hotel Peristil ££
Beautifully built boutique hotel incorporating elements from Diocletian's Palace and the medieval city of Split. Conservative décor with personal touches.
Poljana kraljise Jelene 5, 21000 Split. Tel: (021) 329 070; fax: (021) 329 088; www.hotelperistil.com
Hotel Vestibul Palace £££
Luxury boutique hotel in Peristil Square in the heart of the Roman Palace, the rooms are ultra-cool, incorporating hi-tech toys yet still

displaying the historic fabric of the building. A beautiful hotel.
Iza Vestibula, 21000 Split. Tel: (021) 329 329; fax: (021) 329 333; www.vestibulpalace.com

Ston
Hotel Ostrea (standard room) ££
Beautiful family-owned hotel overlooking the small harbour at Mali Ston.
Mali Ston, 20230 Ston. Tel: (020) 754 555; fax: (020) 754 575; www.ostrea.hr

Volosko (near Opatija)
Villa Kapetanović ££
New small boutique hotel on the hillside above Volosko. Simple but elegantly furnished rooms and a small spa on site.
Novacesta 12a, Volosko, 51410 Opatija. Tel: (051) 741 355; fax: (051) 741 356; www.villa-kapetanovic.hr

The Hotel Apoksiomen at Mali Lošinj

Zadar
Falkensteiner Funimation ££–£££
Huge complex on the coast outside Zadar, Funimation has everything for a fun family holiday including a new waterpark, entertainment programme and kids' club.
Majstora Radova 7, 23000 Zadar. Tel: (023) 206 636; fax: (023) 332 065; www.falkensteiner.com

Zagreb
Arcotel Allegra £££
The first designer hotel in the capital boasts chic clean lines with a nautical theme and personalised rooms.
Branimirova 29, 10000 Zagreb. Tel: (01) 469 6000; www.arcotel.ac
Palace Hotel £££
Refurbished late 19th-century building right in the heart of town.
Strossmayerov trg 10, 10000 Zagreb. Tel: (01) 4920 530; www.palace.hr
The Regent Esplanade ££££
Grande dame of Zagreb hotels, the neo-classical Esplanade was built in 1925 but has been refurbished to top-class standards. Set in the 'green horseshoe' of parks (*see p47*).
Mihanovićeva 1, 10000 Zagreb. Tel: (01) 456 6666; www.regenthotels.com

A ROOM WITH A VIEW?
If you have a penchant for the unusual, try staying in a lighthouse. There are more than ten to choose from, including two available close to Makarska in northern Dalmatia.
Contact: Plovput, Split. Tel: (021) 390 666; fax: (021) 390 630; www.plovput.hr

Practical guide

Arriving
Entry formalities
Citizens of the following countries can enter Croatia without a visa, provided their stay is for under 90 days: all EU countries, Australia, Canada, New Zealand and the USA. Citizens of other countries should consult the Croatian Embassy in their own country for visa information.

All foreign visitors must register with the police within 48 hours of arrival. If you are staying in a hotel or campsite, they will undertake to register for you.

By air
The main airport of entry is Zagreb. *Tel: (01) 6265 222; www.zagreb-airport.hr*

There are also international flights into Dubrovnik (*tel: (020) 733 377*), Pula (*tel: (052) 530 105*) and Split (*tel: (021) 203 555*) on the Adriatic Coast.

All major European airlines fly scheduled services into Zagreb several times each week, including British Airways (*www.britishairways.com*), Air France (*www.airfrance.com*), and Lufthansa (*www.lufthansa.com*). Croatia Airlines (*www.croatiaairlines.hr*) is the national carrier offering a network of services to major cities throughout Europe.

Budget airlines are now also providing flights. easyJet (*www.easyjet.com*) flies to Rijeka from London Luton and Bristol and to Split from London Gatwick, while Ryanair (*www.ryanair.com*) has a service to Pula from London Stansted. You can also get to Split and Zagreb from London Luton with Wizz Air (*www.wizzair.com*). Fly Thomas Cook (*www.flythomascook.com*) offers services to Pula and Split (summer only) from London Gatwick and Manchester.

There are no direct flights to Croatia from the USA, Canada, Australia or New Zealand. Multiple ticket combinations for flights into Europe and onward to Zagreb or the Adriatic airports are possible, so it's best to consult a travel agent about the cheapest or most convenient route.

Charter flights are available in summer to Split, Dubrovnik, Pula and Hvar as part of a package tour. Some companies may be happy to offer a flight-only deal, but it's also advisable to check prices of flight/hotel packages, as these may offer better value than booking separate flights and hotels. Thomas Cook (*www.thomascook.com*) offers packages, or check other quality holiday companies.

By coach
Eurolines (*www.eurolines.co.uk*) runs several services per week from locations

in the UK to Croatia, though this may involve transfers. The journey takes at least three days.

By rail

There are services to Zagreb from Milan, Venice or Trieste in Italy, Munich and Leipzig in Germany, and Vienna and Salzburg in Austria. All these cities link to the greater western European rail network. For a full range of options and other details, contact European Rail (*www.europeanrail.com*).

By road

There is easy road access to Croatia across northern Italy and the northeastern corner of Slovenia into Istria. From the UK allow four full days of travel. Make sure you carry the car's registration document and have insurance cover for the vehicle – this may involve getting a Green Card extension to your normal insurance policy. You may be asked to document any existing damage to your vehicle when you enter Croatia.

By sea

There are several vehicle ferry services from Croatia to Italy (the ports of Ancona, Bari, Pescara and Trieste). The Croatian line Jadrolinija offers services year-round from Ancona to Split and Zadar along with Bari to Dubrovnik. *Tel: (051) 666 111; www.jadrolinija.hr.* SEM Maritime Lines (*www. splittours.hr*) offers a year-round Split

Welcome to Croatia

to Ancona service, as does the Italian company Adriatica Navigazione (*www.gruppotirrenia.it/adriatica*), who also run a summer Linea della Costa Istriana, linking Italian ports with ports in northern Croatia.

Camping

Facilities are excellent, especially along the Adriatic coast, where large sites occupy exceptional beach-side locations and resemble mini-resorts. Sites get very crowded during the summer school holidays, when a reservation is recommended. Most campsites close in winter (Oct–Apr).

For more information explore the Croatian Camping Union website at www.camping.hr or contact The Caravan Club in the UK (www.caravanclub.co.uk).

Children

Stocks of essentials such as nappies and baby food can be found in towns all across Croatia, but you may have problems finding child-friendly changing places. Highchairs in restaurants are nonexistent outside the major package-tour hotels.

In the summer, make sure you protect them against the strong sun.

Mosquitoes may be a problem, so take insect repellent.

Don't allow children to play with animals: rabies, though not common, is a problem.

Check for ticks after summer hikes. They can occasionally carry diseases such as rabies. If a tick is found, do not pull it from the body as mouth parts can be left in the flesh and become infected. Using tweezers, take a firm hold of the tick's head until it lets go. Alternatively, travel quickly to a pharmacy or doctor's surgery to have the creature removed.

Climate

The Croatian climate is characterised by hot and dry summers and cool-to-cold damp winters.

On the coast, temperatures are tempered in summer by breezes off the Adriatic, whilst in winter the same water mass keeps temperatures slightly higher on the coast than inland.

Crime

When you visit Croatia you'll be at a relatively low risk of being a victim of serious crime. However, so-called petty crime such as theft can be a problem in big cities or on the coast, especially theft from vehicles.

Take the following precautions to minimise your chances of a loss.

Do not leave valuables in a car, and leave nothing on show.

Don't carry large amounts of cash or valuables with you.

Deposit valuables in the hotel safe.

Take care at cashpoint machines.

Always carry handbags over your shoulder and across your chest to thwart bag-snatchers.

Don't leave valuables unattended on the beach or in cafés and restaurants.

Customs regulations

Foreigners over 16 are allowed to take in the following items duty free:
200 cigarettes or 100 cigarillos or 50 cigars or 250g (8³/₄ oz) of loose tobacco
1 litre (1³/₄ pt) spirits
1 litre (1³/₄ pt) port, sherry or champagne
2 litres (3¹/₂ pt) table wine

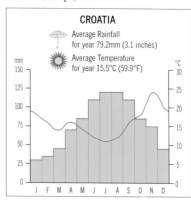

CROATIA

Average Rainfall
for year 79.2mm (3.1 inches)

Average Temperature
for year 15.5°C (59.9°F)

mm   °C
150   30
125   25
100   20
75   15
50   10
25   5
0   0
  J F M A M J J A S O N D

50g (1³/₄ oz) of perfume
250g (8³/₄ oz) of eau de toilette
Croatian currency to the value of
15,000kn may be imported or exported
without restriction.

Although unlimited personal effects
can be temporarily imported (i.e. for
the duration of your trip), you should
declare any high-value items such as
expensive cameras or computers.

Croatian currency up to the amount
of 2,000 kuna may be exported without
restriction.

Driving

Croatia drives on the right, overtaking
on the left. Road signs conform with
European standards, but road conditions
are mixed, with care needed on some
minor roads – not all damage sustained
during the war has been repaired,
especially in the east, and there was little
regular maintenance for well over a
decade. The main Adriatic coastal
highway carries a great deal of holiday
and commercial traffic, so pay particular
attention when travelling here. A toll
motorway linking Zagreb with Split is
now open, extending to Dubrovnik in
the near future.

Speed limits for cars are 130km/h
(80mph) on motorways, 100km/h
(62mph) on arterial routes, 90km/h
(55mph) on main roads outside urban
areas and 50km/h (30mph) in urban
areas. Seat belts are compulsory for
driver and front-seat passenger, and
helmets compulsory for motorcyclists.

The blood-alcohol limit is 0.0 per cent

and it is strictly enforced. So no alcohol
should be found in a driver's blood.

Children under 12 should be seated
in the back of vehicles.

Driving with headlights is obligatory
night and day.

There are a number of toll roads.

The website of the Croatian
Automobile Association provides
information on many aspects of
motoring in Croatia at *www.hak.hr*

Car rental

Cars can be rented in Zagreb and in all
the resorts and towns.

The international car rental
companies have new vehicles, but may
charge more than a local agency. Renting
through a local agency will be cheaper,
and cars are generally of good quality. If
you wish to travel extensively in Croatia,
a local company may not offer as good a
back-up service as an international
company if you break down some
distance from the rental office.

Your domestic driving licence is
recognised in Croatia. You will need to
have had a full licence for at least one
year and be over 21 to rent a vehicle.

The Croatian Auto Club (*Hrvatski
Autoklub, www.hak.hr, with info in
English*) has an emergency service
number of 987, but operators do not
speak English.

Electricity

Croatia uses 220V for its supply. Plugs
are the two-pin variety, so travellers
from the UK will need an adaptor.

Embassies

All foreign embassies in Croatia have offices in the capital, Zagreb.

Australian Embassy
Kaptol Centar 3
kat Nova Ves 11/III
10000 Zagreb
Tel: (01) 489 1200;
fax: (01) 48 91 216;
www.auembassy.hr

Canadian Embassy
Prilaz Gjure Deželića 4
10000 Zagreb
Tel: (01) 4881 211;
fax: (01) 4881 230.

Republic of Ireland Honorary Consulate
Miramarska 23 (Eurocenter), 10000 Zagreb. Tel: (01) 6310 025; fax: (01) 2413 901.

New Zealand Consulate
Vlaska ulica 50A, 10000 Zagreb.
Tel/fax: (01) 6151 382.

UK
Ivana Lučića 4 10000 Zagreb
Tel: (01) 6009 100; fax: (01) 6009 111;
www.fco.gov.uk

Honorary Consul
Obala Hrvatskog Narodnog Preporoda 10/III
21000 Split
Tel: (021) 346 007; fax: (021) 362 905.

Honorary Consul
Bunićeva Poljana 3
20000 Dubrovnik
Tel/fax: (020) 324 597.

US Embassy
Ulica Thomasa Jeffersona 2, Buzin
10010 Zagreb
Tel: (01) 661 2200; fax: (01) 6658 933;
www.usembassy.hr

The main road system is clearly signposted

Emergency telephone numbers

Fire

Tel: 93

Ambulance

Tel: 94

Police

Tel: 92

Health

There are no compulsory inoculations for travel to Croatia.

There is basic health care (a clinic) in most small towns, with hospitals in major towns. Standards are high, doctors are well trained and most speak some English.

Emergency treatment for all citizens and visitors is free. UK and EU citizens will not be charged for other forms of health care. UK citizens should show their passports to obtain treatment. Other EU citizens must carry an appropriate form (contact your own government for details). Citizens of other countries must pay at time of treatment in local currency (take receipts to claim money back from your insurance company), according to a list of prices published by the Croatian government.

Pharmacies sell many drugs over the counter; however, brand names vary, so if you need a specific medication/drug, take an empty packet with you to aid the pharmacist, or carry a prescription from your doctor.

Several minor nuisances should be watched for. Ticks are found in the grassland of country areas and National Parks. They should be removed

carefully using tweezers (*see p180*). Snakes will usually avoid humans but there are poisonous species, so be vigilant in remote areas. Spiky sea urchins can inflict wounds on swimmers, snorkellers or divers – if their spines become embedded in the skin, remove carefully, as they can become infected. Mosquitoes can be a problem, so carry repellent and cover arms and legs in the evenings. The sun can be strong, so protect yourself properly.

Insurance

Having adequate insurance cover is vital. UK citizens and other EU nationals will be treated without charge in Croatia, but a travel insurance policy will allow repatriation if the injuries or illness warrants it.

You should take a European Health Insurance Card (EHIC) with you when you go; this can be obtained, free of charge, through most UK post offices or through the UK Department of Health via their website (*www.dh.gov.uk*) or by telephoning *0845 6062030* (from outside the UK call *(0044) 191 203555).*

All other nationalities should ensure adequate cover for illness, as they will be charged at point of treatment (though prices are not extortionate and are on a set national scale). Travellers should always have cover for everything they carry with them in case of loss or theft. Insurance companies also usually provide cover for cancellation or travel delay in their policies. Though not essential, this offers some compensation if travel plans go awry.

Language

The national language of Croatia is *Hrvatski.*

PRONUNCIATION

All letters are pronounced as in English unless indicated below.

Capital	Lower case	Pronunciation
C	c	'ts' as in its
Č	č	'ch' as in chips
Ć	ć	't'
Đ	đ	'dg' as is lodge
G	g	hard 'g' as in go
J	j	'y' as in yes
Š	š	'sh' as in shout
Ž	ž	'zh' as the s in treasure
Aj	aj	pronounced as the 'igh' in night

Lost property

Airports and large railway stations have lost-property departments, or try the local police station. You'll need an official police report to make an insurance claim for any lost property. If you lose your passport, contact your embassy or consulate immediately.

Maps

For touring, Euromap produces a detailed, though rather large, 'Croatia and Slovenia' map, ISBN 3-575-03108-8.

Media

Croatian state television has three channels; RTL and Nova TV are two further, commercial, national channels. Imported programmes are shown in the original language with subtitles. Large hotels have satellite, which usually provide CNN and BBC News 24 channels. Croatian Radio offers three national channels with eight regional stations scattered across the country. There are three commercial stations, Radio 101, Otvoreni Radio and Narodno Radio.

There are no English-language newspapers printed in Croatia, though there are several websites with pertinent current affairs info in English, the best being HINA (*www.hina.hr*), with Croatian current affairs reported and discussed. International press is available in Zagreb and in resorts along the coast, but these may be one day old.

Internet cafés are common and access is cheap.

Money matters
Credit cards

Credit cards are not universally accepted across Croatia, but their use is gaining ground. If you intend to stay in the capital or on the Adriatic coast you'll find their use more widespread, but it's still better to ask beforehand at restaurants and petrol stations if you intend to pay with a card (some have window stickers but don't actually have card facilities). It is also wise to carry enough cash to cover your daily needs, just in case.

You can use your credit card to get cash advances over the counter in some banks.

Here are a few helpful phrases:

English	Phonetic pronunciation	Spelling
hello	dobar dan	dobar dan
goodbye	doveedenya	doviđenja
yes	daa	da
no	ney	ne
please	moleem vas	molim vas
thank you	hvahlah	hvala
Do you speak English?	govoreetey lee engleskee	Gove(o)rite li a(e)ngleski?
I don't understand	Nay razoomeeyem	Ne razumijem
Where is/are...?	Gdyey yey/soo	Gdje je/su...?
bank	bankah	banka
museum	moozey	muzej
post office	poshta	Pošta
toilet	vay tsey	WC
tourist office	tooreesteechkey oored	turistički ured
How much is it?	Koliko ovo koshta	Koliko ovo košta
Monday	Ponedyelyak	Ponedjeljak
Tuesday	Ootorak	Utorak
Wednesday	Sreeyeda	Srijeda
Thursday	Chetvrtak	Četvrtak
Friday	Petak	Petak
Saturday	Soobota	Subota
Sunday	Nedyelya	Nedjelja
one	yedan	jedan
two	dvah	dva
three	tree	tri
four	cheteeree	četiri
five	pet	pet
six	shest	šest
seven	sedam	sedam
eight	osam	osam
nine	devet	devet
ten	deset	deset
one hundred	stoh	sto
help!	pomoch	pomoč

Money

Croatian currency is the *kuna* (abbreviated at bureaux de change and banks as 'HRK' but locally in shops as 'kn'). One kuna is made up of 100 lipa with note denominations of 5, 10, 20, 50, 100, 200, 500 and 1000 kuna and coins of 1, 2, 5, 10, 20 and 50 lipa and 1, 2, 5 and 25 kuna (often issued as special edition or commemorative coins).

Foreign currency can be exchanged at banks and bureaux de change, which are plentiful at resorts and in major towns. Travellers will find it easier if they carry US dollars, euros or pounds sterling, which will be easier to change than other currencies.

Traveller's cheques are not as easy to cash as foreign currency. However, the advantage of them is that they are more secure than cash, as you can get them replaced if they are lost or stolen.

ATMs are numerous, and you will certainly be able to get cash in Zagreb and the Adriatic resorts. Before you travel, check that your bank has an agreement with the banking system in Croatia.

Opening hours

Normal business hours are Mon–Fri 8.30am–4.30pm. Government offices will close for an hour at lunchtime (anytime between noon and 2pm), but commercial organisations will generally stay open.

Shops open Mon–Fri 8am–8pm, but have extended hours in summer, especially on the Adriatic coast. Some may close at lunchtime for a siesta during the heat of the afternoon.

Main post offices are open Mon–Fri 7am–7pm but open later on the Adriatic coast during the summer. Smaller offices open 7am–2pm. On Saturday there will generally be a duty post office open.

Large banks are open Mon–Fri 7am–7pm, Sat 8am–1pm. In smaller towns, opening hours are Mon–Fri 8am–noon and 3–7pm, Sat 8am–noon.

Museums are generally open from 10am–5.00pm, and longer in the evenings mid-July–mid-Sept, but they will be closed for at least one day a week. Many also close at lunchtimes for one hour. Opening times for all museums are prone to change, and provincial museums may not adhere to the opening hours on the door (i.e. have longer lunch-hours than printed and different closing days).

Pharmacies open from 8am–1pm and 3–7pm.

Police

Police (*policija*) wear navy-blue uniforms and routinely carry sidearms. They are generally approachable for queries such as asking directions.

In an emergency, telephone 92.

Post offices

Postal services are operated by the state-run HP, recognisable by their yellow signs and postboxes. Post offices are open Mon–Fri 7am–7pm (in major cities until 10pm) and Sat

7am–1pm. Newsagents and souvenir shops will also sell stamps (*marka*) for postcards.

Public holidays

The following dates are official holidays in Croatia. All government buildings and banks will be closed, but not all commercial businesses.

1 January	**New Year's Day**
6 January	**Epiphany**
March/April	**Good Friday and Easter Sunday**
1 May	**Labour Day**
22 June	**Anti-Fascist Victory Day**
27 June	**Statehood Day**
5 August	**Victory Day**
15 August	**Assumption Day**
8 October	**Independence Day**
1 November	**All Saints' Day**
25/26 December	**Christmas**

Public transport

Air

There is a small domestic air network with flights between Zagreb and Dubrovnik, Split, Pula, Rijeka and Brac.
www.croatiaairlines.hr

Buses

Bus services are run by private companies, and offer an efficient method of touring. Several large companies operate integrated systems across the whole country including Croatia Bus (*www.croatiabus.hr*). Other local companies provide a more limited service, including Contus (*www.contus.hr*) with services between Zadar, Split and Dubrovnik, and Promet-Split (*www.promet-split.hr*). For more details look on the Visit Croatia website (*www.visit-croatia.co.uk*).

Ferries are still a vital means of transport in Croatia

Practical guide

Ferries

A well-managed fleet of ferries links the mainland to the islands year-round, supplemented by a seasonal flotilla of smaller pleasure boats. Jadrolinija (*www.jadrolinija.hr*) has the largest fleet, and plies the whole intercoastal waterway on the Adriatic, linking all the major islands. The local tourist office or harbourmaster's office will have details of local ferries and summer boat connections from their coastal towns. (*See the appropriate* Destination guide *sections for further details.*)

Rail

All rail tracks damaged during the war have been repaired, and the rail system is a useful way of getting around the major towns. Croatian Railways runs decent services (though there is no connection with Dubrovnik and southern Dalmatia) and their website, *www.hznet.hr*, offers a journey-planning option in English. Pricing is not always available, however.

Sustainable tourism

Thomas Cook is a strong advocate of ethical and fairly traded tourism and believes that the travel experience should be as good for the places visited as it is for the people who visit them. That's why we firmly support The Travel Foundation, a charity that develops solutions to help improve and protect holiday destinations, their environment, traditions and culture. To find out what you can do to make a positive difference to the places you travel to and the people who live there, please visit *www.thetravelfoundation.org.uk*

Telephones

Modern hotels will usually have a direct-dial phone system – but beware, as they often add extortionate surcharges on calls. Ask about charges before you pick up the phone.

The country code for Croatia is 385.

The following are country codes for international calls from Croatia.

Australia 00 61
Ireland 00 353
New Zealand 00 64
UK 00 44
USA and Canada 00 1

Croatia Telecom is the main provider, though the recent opening up of the telecommunications market to other companies will mean more competition in the future.

Time

Croatia is one hour ahead of Greenwich Mean Time, so if it is midday in Zagreb it is 11am in London, and 6am in New York and Toronto.

Croatia operates summer time or daylight saving time, and its clocks are advanced one hour between late March and late September.

Tipping

A 10 per cent service charge is normal at restaurants. It is included in the price, when it is then considered reasonable to leave any coins returned with your change. Round up the charge in taxis and leave small change in bars. Porters should receive 5 kuna or so for each bag.

Toilets

Toilets are generally of the sit-down variety and are usually clean. There is a small charge for public toilets. Those in cafés and bars are free, but you are expected to be a client to use them.

Tourist information

Every town and city has a well-equipped and helpful tourist information office that will help with information, excursions and accommodation. For information before you depart, contact the following offices of the Croatian National Tourist Office.

UK

2 The Lanchesters
162–164 Fulham Palace Road
London W6 9ER
Tel: 020 8563 7979
Fax: 020 8563 2616
www.gb.croatia.hr

USA

350 Fifth Avenue, Suite 4003
New York
NY 10118
Tel: 212 279 8672
Fax: 212 279 8683
www.us.croatia.hr

For all other countries the head office of the National Tourist Office is at

Importanne Galleria
Iblerov trg 10/IV
10000 Zagreb
Tel: (00 385) 1 4699 333
Fax: (00 385) 1 4557 827.

The tourist board website *www.croatia.hr* has comprehensive information in English.

Croatian Angels provides tourist information throughout Croatia, and internationally, from 23 Mar–15 Oct from 9am–5pm on *tel: 062 999 999.*

The Croatian Tourist Board supplies information on the VIP mobile telephone network. Dial 7799. Call charges apply.

Visit Croatia has an excellent website – *www.visitcroatia.co.uk* – with lots of background information on the different regions of the country, plus practical facts to help you plan your trip. You could also try official local sites such as *www.zagreb-touristinfo.hr*, *www.istra.com*, *www.tz-dubrovnik.hr* and *www.visitsplit.com*

Travellers with disabilities

Provision for travellers with mobility problems is poor, though new buildings have to meet a code standard for wheelchair access. Always make specific enquiries with hotels if you require specially equipped rooms. Holiday Care Services has holiday and travel information for people with disabilities. *Tel: 0845 124 9971 (UK);* *www.holidaycare.org.uk*

Index

Acknowledgements

Thomas Cook wishes to thank the photographers, picture libraries and other organisations for the loan of the photographs reproduced in this book, to whom copyright in the photographs belongs.

FLICKR/Beatdrifter 114, Leo the Lop 129; FOTOLIA/Nicolas Auvinet 103, Marco Bottarelli 161, Yanik Chauvin 149, Dubravko Grakalic 4, Werner Hilpe 7, Joyful Girl 167, 187, Robert Lerich 23, Thibaut Oger 107, Iva Villi 33, 67, 110, WIKIMEDIA COMMONS/Donarreiskoffer 143, Zoran Knez & Dražen Radujkov 84, WORLD PICTURES/Photoshot 1, 52, 94, 104, 139, 151, 159, 171, 172, 173.

All remaining photos were taken by Pete Bennett.

Proofreading: JAN McCANN for CAMBRIDGE PUBLISHING MANAGEMENT LTD

SEND YOUR THOUGHTS TO
BOOKS@THOMASCOOK.COM

We're committed to providing the very best up-to-date information in our travel guides and constantly strive to make them as useful as they can be. You can help us to improve future editions by letting us have your feedback. If you've made a wonderful discovery on your travels that we don't already feature, if you'd like to inform us about recent changes to anything that we do include, or if you simply want to let us know your thoughts about this guidebook and how we can make it even better – we'd love to hear from you.

Send us ideas, discoveries and recommendations today and then look out for your valuable input in the next edition of this title. And, as an extra 'thank you' from Thomas Cook Publishing, you'll be automatically entered into our exciting prize draw.

Emails to the above address, or letters to Travellers Project Editor, Thomas Cook Publishing, PO Box 227, Coningsby Road, Peterborough PE3 8SB, UK.

Please don't forget to let us know which title your feedback refers to!